# Economic Interdependence and Development in East Asia

# Economic Interdependence and Development in East Asia

---■---

*Hans C. Blomqvist*

PRAEGER

Westport, Connecticut
London

**Library of Congress Cataloging-in-Publication Data**

Blomqvist, H. C. (Hans-Christer)
  Economic interdependence and development in East Asia / Hans C.
Blomqvist.
    p.  cm.
  Includes bibliographical references and index.
  ISBN 0–275–95583–4 (alk. paper)
  1. East Asia—Economic conditions.  2. East Asia—Economic
integration.  I. Title.
  HC460.5.B57  1997
  330.95′04—dc20        96–44676

British Library Cataloguing in Publication Data is available.

Library of Congress Catalog Card Number: 96–44676
ISBN: 0–275–95583–4

First published in 1997

Praeger Publishers, 88 Post Road West, Westport, CT  06881
An imprint of Greenwood Publishing Group, Inc.

Printed in the United States of America

The paper used in this book complies with the
Permanent Paper Standard issued by the National
Information Standards Organization (Z39.48–1984).

10 9 8 7 6 5 4 3 2 1

**Copyright Acknowledgments**

The author and publisher gratefully acknowledge permission to use the following material by Hans
C. Blomqvist:

Chapter 2 is a slightly revised version of "The 'Flying Geese' Model of Regional Development: A
Constructive Interpretation," *Journal of Asia Pacific Economy* 1, no. 2 (October 1996). Reprinted
with the permission of Routledge Journals.

Chapter 4 is a revised version of "Determinants of Bilateral Trade Flows in East Asia." In *Economic
Reforms, Liberalization and Trade in the Asia-Pacific Region.* Edited by D. T. Nguyen and K. C.
Roy. Copyright 1994. Reprinted with the permission of New Age International (P) Limited, Publish-
ers (formerly Wiley Eastern), New Delhi.

Excerpts in Chapter 5 from "Intraregional Foreign Investment in East Asia," *ASEAN Economic Bulletin* 11, no. 3 (March 1995). Reproduced here with the kind permission of the publisher, Institute of
Southeast Asian Studies, Singapore.

Excerpts in Chapter 6 and Chapter 7 from "ASEAN as a Model for Third World Regional Economic
Co-operation?" *ASEAN Economic Bulletin* 10, no. 1 (July 1993). Reproduced here with the kind
permission of the publisher, Institute of Southeast Asian Studies, Singapore.

*To the memory of my mother*

# Contents

# Abbreviations

| | |
|---|---|
| ADB | Asian Development Bank |
| ADPS | ASEAN Dialogue Partner System |
| AFTA | ASEAN Free Trade Area |
| AIC | ASEAN Industrial Complementation |
| AIJV | ASEAN Industrial Joint Venture |
| AIP | ASEAN Industrial Projects |
| APEC | Asia-Pacific Economic Cooperation |
| ASEAN | Association of Southeast Asian Nations |
| BBC | Brand-to-Brand Complementation Agreement |
| CEPT | Common Effective Preferential Tariff |
| EAEC | East Asian Economic Caucus |
| EAEG | East Asian Economic Group |
| EC | European Communities |
| ECAFE | Economic Commission for Asia and the Far East |
| ESCAP | Economic and Social Commission for Asia and the Pacific |
| FDI | Foreign Direct Investment |
| GATS | General Agreement on Trade in Services |
| GATT | General Agreement on Tariffs and Trade |
| GDP | Gross Domestic Product |
| GSP | General System of Preferences |
| HS | Harmonized System |
| IPR | Institute of Pacific Relations |
| ISEAS | Institute of Southeast Asian Studies |
| LDC | Less Developed Country |
| MITI | Ministry of International Trade and Industry |
| MNC | Multinational Corporation |
| NAFTA | North American Free Trade Area |
| NBER | National Bureau of Economic Research |
| NIE | Newly Industrialized Economy |

| | |
|---|---|
| ODA | Official Development Aid |
| OECD | Organisation for Economic Co-operation and Development |
| OPTAD | Organization for Pacific Trade, Aid, and Development |
| PAFTA | Pacific Free Trade Area |
| PAFTAD | Pacific Trade and Development Conference |
| PBEC | Pacific Basin Economic Council |
| PECC | Pacific Economic Cooperation Council |
| PTA | Preferential Trading Arrangement |
| SITC | Standardized International Trade Classification |
| WTO | World Trade Organization |

# Preface

This book is the end result of a long process. When I began teaching development economics in 1984, I soon realized that any successful study of the subject requires case studies of specific countries or regions. Since studying successful cases of development seems more inspiring than looking into unsuccessful ones—although the lessons to be learned from the latter no doubt would be equally valuable—my interest drifted more and more toward the Asia-Pacific region and especially to East Asia which, of course, is an unprecedented example of rapid development. One of the reasons for this appears to be the high degree of complementarity and interdependence in this region. This came to be the focus of this book.

I am grateful to several institutions and people for facilitating the work leading to the present volume. I would like to thank the Academy of Finland for financing a one-year leave of absence and the Hans Bang Foundation for sponsoring another three months' leave. I had the privilege of spending the first of these leaves at the Institute of Southeast Asian Studies (ISEAS) in Singapore, a unique and outstanding environment for anyone doing research on Southeast and East Asia. Part of the other leave I spent at ISEAS as well, and the rest of that time at the Department of Economics, University of Queensland in Brisbane, also a conducive place for research on East Asia. Some basic theoretical foundations of the work were conceived during a stay with the Americas Program at Stanford University, in the United States. I am very grateful to these institutions for providing me with working accommodations and other facilities as well as to the Swedish School of Economics and Business Administration in Helsinki and Vasa, Finland, for providing me with excellent working conditions during other periods.

It is impossible to mention all the colleagues and friends who have somehow contributed ideas and comments relevant to the work on this book. I would like to thank Tilak Doshi, Mats Lundahl, Mya Than, Ng Chee Yuen, Tom Nguyen,

Clark Reynolds, Kartik C. Roy, Joseph Tan, Clem Tisdell, and many others for inspiring discussions on issues pertaining to the work. I would also like to thank my wife, Clara, and my grown-up children Anna-Clara and Johan for cheerfully bearing with my long spells of absence from home during the work on this book.

# Economic Interdependence and Development in East Asia

# 1

## The New Global Powerhouse: Overview and Outline of the Issues

### INTRODUCTION

For several decades now, East Asia has been developing faster than any other part of the world. To begin with, the strong growth rates were confined to some of the countries in the region, in particular to Japan and the so-called Asian newly industrialized economies (NIEs):[1] Hong Kong, Singapore, South Korea,[2] and Taiwan. Then other countries jumped on the bandwagon, and today the whole region, with a few minor exceptions, belongs to the group of rapidly developing economies. This has led to a strong shift in global trade and investment patterns and is bound to lead to a restructuring of global political power and security systems, too, a development that is already well under way.

It is no exaggeration to maintain that these changes are the most important developments of the twentieth century in the economic realm. They are also a source of uncertainty and friction, however, as development of one region has inevitable repercussions on, for instance, the industrial and employment structure of other regions. Hence the emerging powerhouses in East Asia have been looked upon with a certain amount of suspicion by politicians and the business community. In the more popular literature on the subject, the emerging Asian economic power has been characterized as a "threat," or at least a "challenge," or, on a more positive note, a "miracle." The tremendous potential benefits for the world economy emanating from such a dynamic region have not always been fully realized.

In the economics profession, the rapidly developing Asian countries have caused mixed reactions and confusion, too. Some authors have even hesitated to recognize as "genuine" the development that has taken place, trying to find weak spots in the process or at least snags that will eventually bring the process to a halt (for a recent example, see Krugman 1994). Sometimes the experience of the dynamic Asian countries has been considered an anomaly, a "special case." By and large, however, the economics profession—like several others—has benefited inasmuch as research on the reasons behind the success has contributed to the progress of the discipline. Most economists by now acknowledge the achievements of the East Asian economies, although many—including myself— hesitate to speak of a "miracle."

An interesting feature of the recent development patterns of East and Southeast Asia is that fairly distinct groups of countries can be discerned as far as their general level of development is concerned. The regional leader, Japan, is followed by the four NIEs. The members of the Association of Southeast Asian Nations (ASEAN), minus Singapore and Vietnam, make up a third group after which come China and the rest of Southeast Asia. Hence countries belonging to both the poorest and the richest groups in the world are represented.

This peculiar regional structure seems to have a certain significance for the fact that the intraregional economic interdependence has increased during the last few decades. The latter development, in turn, has made the region much more resilient than before to cyclical fluctuations in the world economy. This can be seen from gross domestic product (GDP) growth figures which demonstrate, on the one hand, that economic growth in East Asia has far outstripped that of the rest of the world, and, on the other, that the correlation between growth in East Asia and the rest of the world has been falling consistently since the early 1970s. For the period 1975–1993 the correlation coefficient between the growth rates in the gross national products in East Asia and the Organisation for Economic Co-operation and Development (OECD) was 0.465 (note, however, that Japan is a heavyweight member in both groups), and between East Asia and the United States, 0.225. The correlation coefficient between the growth rates of the United States and the OECD, in turn, was 0.896.

The increasing regional interdependence also seems to be one of several possible explanations for the rapid growth itself inasmuch as the regional interaction appears to have facilitated economic restructuring. As it is, of course, extremely unlikely that a cluster of rapidly growing countries would emerge at random, one explanation for the phenomenon has been spillover effects from one country to another (Easterly 1995). Despite increasing regional interdependence, a popular conception is still that the East Asian economies are propelled mainly by developments in the Western industrialized countries (Kwan 1994: 1–4).

Table 1.1 gives some basic macroeconomic facts on the economies dealt with in this book, and Figure 1.1 depicts the fluctuations in the region's economic activity compared to the global developments.

The group consisting of Japan, the NIEs, and ASEAN today produces about one-fourth of the global GDP (of which Japan stands for 18 percent), up from a marginal 9 percent in 1960. In terms of foreign trade the change is even more impressive: for exports the figures are 26 and 5.4 percent, respectively (World Bank, *World Development Report* 1995; Government of the Republic of China, *Monthly Bulletin of Statistics of the Republic of China* 1995; Elek 1991). Much of this trade is intraregional, as is shown below. A recent World Bank publication (World Bank 1994: 2) notes that the (nominal) value of exports from the region increased more than thirtyfold during the last twenty-five years, that is, since the late 1960s. According to a forecast made in the same study, East

**Table   1.1**
**Basic   Macroeconomic   Data   on   East   Asia**

| Country | GDP US$ (billions) | GDP Growth 1980–93 % | GNP/cap. 1993 US$ | Exports 1993 US$ (billions) | Gross Savings/ GNP % | Gross Capital Formation/ GDP % |
|---------|-----|-----|-----|-----|-----|-----|
| Japan | 4,214.2 | 4.0 | 31,490 | 362.6 | 33 | 30 |
| Korea | 330.8 | 9.1 | 7,660 | 83.5 | 35 | 34 |
| Taiwan | 214.0 | 8.1 | 10566 | 84.9 | 28 | 24 |
| Hong Kong | 90.0 | 6.5 | 18,060 | 135.0 | 31 | 27 |
| China | 425.6 | 9.6 | 490 | 91.6 | 40 | 41 |
| Brunei | 4.2 | -0.2 | 18,500 | 2.4 | 35 | .. |
| Indonesia | 144.7 | 5.8 | 740 | 36.8 | 31 | 28 |
| Malaysia | 64.5 | 6.2 | 3,140 | 47.1 | 33 | 33 |
| Philippines | 54.1 | 1.4 | 850 | 11.3 | 16 | 24 |
| Singapore | 55.1 | 6.9 | 19,850 | 74.1 | 48 | 44 |
| Thailand | 124.9 | 8.2 | 2,110 | 37.1 | 36 | 40 |
| Vietnam | 12.8 | .. | 170 | 3.0 | 16 | 21 |
| **Total** | 23,112.6 | n.a. | n.a. | 969.4 | n.a. | n.a. |

*Note:* n.a. = not available.

*Sources:*  Compiled from World Bank, *World Development Report* 1995 and *World Tables* 1995;
        ASEAN 1995, Government of the Republic of China, *Monthly Statistics of the Republic of
        China,* July 1994.

Asia will account for two-fifths of incremental global purchasing power and
between one-third and one-half of incremental imports between 1992–2000,
figures that underline the tremendous importance of this region already in the
immediate future, and even more so in the longer run. As for foreign direct
investment (FDI), the region was the source of 25 percent of the global flow in
1990 (Urata 1993), a considerable proportion of which was intraregional. As a
recipient, "developing" Asia (the NIEs but not Japan included) absorbed 19
percent of the global FDI flow of $US 158 billion in 1992, which is 58 percent
of the flow to all developing countries (UNCTAD 1994). A very large part—but
quite variable between the different countries—comprised investment from
within the region, predominantly but not entirely, from the Asian NIEs and
Japan.

   As noted by Bradford and Branson (1987: 3), the Asian-Pacific region provides
a fascinating "laboratory" for studying the dynamics of economic growth because
of its rapid development during the last few decades. The fact that the countries
in the region are also very disparate in most respects except for their impressive
economic development, provides an even richer, although confusing, basis for
research. The potential lessons for other developing countries as well as for
students of development economics cannot be exaggerated.

   Still, these lessons are far from clear-cut. According to a striking analogy by
Riedel (1988: 2–3), economic development can be compared to a combination
lock where all tumblers have to fall into place until the lock can be  opened. The

**Figure 1.1**
**GNP Growth Rates in East Asia and the World, 1975–1993**

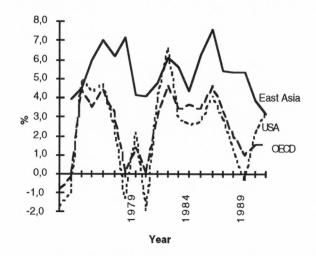

*Note:* Japan is part of both East Asia and the OECD, whereas the United States is a member of the OECD.
*Source:* Compiled from World Bank, *World Tables* 1995.

set of tumblers may not always be identical and the combination may not always be the same, however. The size, the political system, and the industrial policy stance of the economies in the region differ widely, and so do their cultural, ethnic, and religious "infrastructure." The only thing in common appears to be a certain degree of outward orientation combined with a relative absence of seriously distorting government interventions. Despite this, most East Asian governments have been far from laissez-faire. On the contrary, many of them have chosen to exercise close control of the development process. Even in that respect, however, variations have been considerable over time and across countries.

Much of the discourse actually dealing with the phenomenon of "Asian dynamism" is geared toward the possibilities or lack of possibilities to envisage an "Asian model of development." Although a good deal of the literature seems to exploit the feeling of uneasiness among many Westerners in the face of emerging competition, and often is somewhat sensation oriented in its approach, there is much serious discussion as well. Apart from the debate on the virtues of outward orientation versus import substitution—where the East Asian countries to a large and increasing extent belong to the former school—most of the debate has evolved about the role of the state versus the market, on the one hand, and about the role of "Asian values," on the other. Puzzlingly, the East Asian experience has been invoked as evidence for both the importance of market-led development and of government intervention. As for the discussion on values—

whether the culture, customs, religions, and so on of Asia may be one of the factors propelling economic development in the region—the answer may be even harder to find, due to the elusive nature of the concepts dealt with. The issue of economic interdependence is also obviously and strongly related to the political and institutional framework.

The purpose of this work is modest compared to the potential field of study, and belongs basically to some aspects of the first of the three topics for debate just outlined: the increasing outward orientation of the economies of the region. The discussion is confined to looking into the interaction between the regional economies through trade and foreign direct investment, relating this to economic growth and development. Some discussion on organized cooperation will also be included.

East Asia, as defined in this book, includes Japan, China, South Korea, Taiwan, Hong Kong, and ASEAN (where Brunei and Vietnam are included in the analyses sporadically because of data problems). Some countries are thus excluded, but this does not affect the general picture conveyed, as these countries are either small or poorly integrated into the region.

## TRADE, INTERDEPENDENCE, AND DEVELOPMENT

Japan, the East Asian NIEs, and several of the members of ASEAN are among the very top countries as far as their shares in world trade are concerned (see International Monetary Fund 1994). These shares have been increasing at a very rapid rate. As a whole, the East Asian countries display large trade surpluses. From a global point of view this is a problem; it is widely believed that these surpluses cannot be sustained in the long run for both economic and political reasons (World Bank 1994). Further liberalization is likely to increase both the intraregional and interregional trade flows still further, however, and the trade surplus may go on growing for some time.

The East Asian countries are important trade partners for each other, and the flows of intraregional direct investment are considerable and increasing. The intraregional trade volumes in the East Asian region are already larger than the trans-Pacific trade flows. Traditional measures indicate increases in openness to trade in the region, sometimes to a quite dramatic extent (cf. Grant, Papadakis, and Richardson 1993: 19).

While the four NIEs embarked on a strategy of export orientation in the early 1960s, the ASEAN countries went on with the early stage of import substitution—that is, substituting domestically produced consumer goods for imports—until the early 1970s. After that the Philippines adopted the "Latin American" strategy of a second stage of import substitution (of intermediate and capital goods), while the others became more outward oriented, although trade barriers remained (cf. Balassa 1991: 11–18). The presence of a large number of multinational companies, trading and investing in the region, and lobbying for reductions in barriers impeding these activities, has probably been instrumental in opening up the economies. Economic de facto integration has, in its turn, been enhanced during the last decade or so by an increasing tendency toward economic liberalization, deregulation, and privatization. The attitude to foreign direct investment, which used to be suspicious or even hostile in many countries, changed radically during the last couple of decades, and today virtually every country has joined the race for procuring as much investment as possible.

A more open economic environment inevitably leads to reallocation of resources, a process that is closely related to changing and increasing trade and investment flows. All this should contribute to increasing efficiency in production and, although it is partly a one-time effect, to higher rates of growth as well. The opening up has been gradual. Japan and the NIEs—especially Hong Kong and Singapore—have been in the lead, and the ASEAN countries Malaysia, the Philippines, and Thailand have followed. Indonesia was the last ASEAN country to embark on this strategy in the mid-1980s. Some of the latter—particularly Indonesia, Thailand, and the Philippines—have carried out reforms in a slightly hesitating manner and with occasional backlashes, and still have considerable trade barriers. This goes for China as well, even though the wave of liberalization has not left that country untouched either. Vietnam is a newcomer in the group and still has a long way to go to catch up with the rest of ASEAN, which it joined in July 1995.

The importance of intraregional trade and other cooperation has been and will be further exacerbated by the opening up of the Chinese economy and, more recently, the Vietnamese economy, which already has led to substantially increased trade flows. The gradual integration of these economies into the region is one of the largest potential sources of continuing growth during the following decades. The proximity of relatively advanced growth centers to China's coastal areas and Vietnam will most probably be of decisive importance in the process. The rest of Southeast Asia, North Korea, and Mongolia are likely to play a minor role in the near future—for different reasons, however.

The increasing trade flows can most readily be interpreted as a consequence of the restructuring taking place according to changing comparative advantages, even though liberalization will, in time, also boost intraindustry trade, which is not determined by comparative advantage. Exchange rate realignments have been important, too, for the changing trade patterns in the Asia-Pacific region during the last decade or so (Kwan 1994: 13–14). This does not change the basic effect of changing comparative advantage, though (Blomqvist 1990).

The Asia-Pacific region is now bound together with an increasingly sophisticated network of trade, investment, and aid connections between countries that both compete with and complement each other. Trade and investment flows of course also interact in an intricate way, but whether investment increases or reduces trade volumes seems to be an empirical question which cannot be answered with the aid of theoretical model analysis.

This intensified economic integration has been achieved without much formalized economic cooperation on the government level. What has actually been there—ASEAN—has often, rightly or wrongly, been played down as an engine of closer integration. The formation of some kind of economic bloc, encompassing parts of or the whole Pacific Rim, has frequently been discussed, however, but the results are still rather inconclusive, even if the formation and subsequent development of the Asia-Pacific Economic Cooperation Forum (APEC) has been seen by some as a first step. As Langhammer (1991a) points out, the Asian Pacific Rim cannot yet be regarded as an integrated area in the usual sense of the term. A factor likely to make things more difficult as far as formalized cooperation is concerned is the fact that the region is more heterogeneous than perhaps any other major region in the world. Moreover, most of the countries in the region have tended to favor nondiscriminating liberalization instead of inward-looking trade blocs.

The apparent reluctance of the East Asian countries notwithstanding, analysts have also pointed to the possible scenario of a more tightly knit East Asian economic trading bloc with Japan—then excluding the Eastern Pacific rim—taking over more and more of the role presently played by the United States.[3] This may happen as a consequence of trade bloc formation in other regions—primarily in North America and Western Europe—but may also develop as a consequence of spontaneous, market-driven, interaction in the East Asian region (cf., e.g., Cronin 1992: 115–118). Much of this interaction is already a fact. The Malaysian proposal of an East Asian Economic Caucus (EAEC) fits well into this picture, even if EAEC is being marketed as a consultative forum, not as an exclusive trade bloc. In this context, the costs and benefits of forming a "yen bloc" have been discussed (see Kwan 1994: ch. 9). On the other hand, the formation of such a regional unit is impeded by the fact that Japan, the only possible leader of such a bloc, is still, for historical reasons, regarded with suspicion by many other Asian countries (cf., for instance, Chen 1993). The country itself has also been extremely reluctant to take on any kind of leadership in the region.

The growing economic interdependence, and the fact that the East Asian region has grown very fast as compared to other parts of the world during the last few decades, prompts the question whether the close interaction between these economies may have something to do with their generally favorable development. The notion of the so-called "Flying Geese" (sometimes—implying more or less the same thing—referred to as a "virtuous circle"; see, e.g., Rana and Dowling 1991) is a theoretical framework suggesting how the mechanisms relating interdependence and national development, and integrating trade and FDI, may work. This model will be employed as the chief theoretical framework in this book.

## FOREIGN DIRECT INVESTMENT

Foreign direct investment is today considered by many observers almost a panacea as far as economic development is concerned. Traditionally, the role of FDI was usually interpreted as that of any capital investment in macroeconomic models, that is, as an instrument for attaining higher productive capacity. As FDI also implies, by definition, that foreign nationals gain influence over the domestic economy and may outcompete domestic firms, foreign investment has not always been welcome in developing countries. Today this attitude has changed completely. With few exceptions, FDI is welcomed with open arms; in fact, foreign firms are often wooed with different incentives aimed at making the host country more attractive. During the last ten years or so, East Asia has been one of the largest recipients of FDI in the world. It should be emphasized, however, that FDI seldom comprises more than a fraction of the host country's capital formation, even if its overall importance may well be much greater due to immaterial benefits (cf. United Nations 1991, 1992a).

As is shown later in this book, an important, if not the only, reason behind the expanding intraregional trade in East Asia has been rapidly expanding intraregional FDI. The significance of foreign direct investment in general and intraregional investment in particular is of rather recent origin in East Asia. Before the 1980s former colonial powers were the major investors in the region, but the magnitude of the investments was not very significant. Today the investments are very large; they are often intraregional and form a tight network binding together the regional economies. At the same time, FDI functions as an instrument for economic restructuring in both home and host countries.

Between 1986 and 1990, developing Asia (including the NIEs) received more than 50 percent of all FDI to developing countries, most of which went to the region under scrutiny in this book (*Transnationals*, December 1991). The growth rate of foreign direct investment in Asia (Japan excluded) has been impressive during the last decade, increasing from US$ 3 billion in 1986 to 19 billion in 1992. The overwhelming part—95 percent in 1989—of the total amount goes to the region discussed here (about 50 percent to the four NIEs, 26 percent to ASEAN, and 19 percent to China). Part of this increase is no doubt due to a diversion effect from, above all, Latin America, where the external debt situation strongly discouraged foreign investment in the 1980s. Increasing Japanese investment, which traditionally has had a clear Asian bias compared to other developed countries, is the main "explanation" for the increase (*Transnationals*, December 1991; World Bank 1994: 41–42).

Japan is still the most important of the intraregional investors, but other countries followed suit in the 1980s. During the last decade or so the FDI situation has changed significantly in that several important new actors have entered the scene. Especially the NIEs have emerged as important investors; in Asia they invest amounts of a similar magnitude as Japan, but they invest heavily in developed countries as well.

The Asian share of investment in the region is on the increase. For example, in 1995, Korea invested more than 50 percent of its overall FDI in Asia, a figure to be compared to one-third five years ago (Leger 1995). The ASEAN countries, China, and India invest in the region as well, although the sums are much smaller in those cases. As a matter of fact, FDI in East Asia is now predominantly (70 percent during 1986–1992) intraregional (World Bank 1994: 43). Moreover, the role of small and medium-sized firms has been on the increase, partly because smaller firms are often subcontractors for the multinational corporations (MNCs) and therefore have an interest in following the latter when they relocate production facilities.

One explanation for the high growth rates is no doubt the trend toward diminishing political risk in Pacific Asia during the last few decades (Andersson and Burenstam Linder 1991). However, it also seems that there has been a difference in the motives for FDI in Asia, as compared to Latin America. In the latter case the aim was to exploit the rents of relatively large home markets protected by an import-substituting foreign trade policy, while in Asia exports, and finding a conducive export base in terms of production capability and production costs, have played a much more significant role (OECD 1987: 32). The level of protection was later lowered in Latin America as well, but the rates of growth have usually been lackluster. Increasingly the growing, if not very protected, markets in Asia have been a lure in themselves (Leger 1995). For more complicated products it is more important to have a firsthand knowledge of the market than when simple, standardized products are concerned.

The volume of FDI is still small compared to intraregional trade. It has been growing rapidly, however, and given that investments may have more profound effects in the long run on the host economies than trade, no proper evaluation of regional interdependence can be done without considering FDI. Besides, FDI will of course affect trade flows, too. Exactly how this will turn out, however, obviously differs depending on the nature of the investment.

Even if the last few decades have seen a surge of theoretical work on FDI, the attempts at integrating trade and FDI theories have to date been rather deficient. This is largely due to the difficulty of integrating important aspects of FDI, such as technology transfer and "ownership advantage" (that is, access to firm-specific unique know-how regarding production technology, management, marketing, and so on) into the models. Instead, versions of the traditional Hecksher-Ohlin model, with mobile capital, have been used. It is, however, questionable whether capital (financial or physical) in itself plays a really significant role in the "package deal" that FDI represents. In most cases the actual capital flows are rather modest in relation to total domestic investment in the host economy. Furthermore, most trade models are static, while the reasons and consequences of FDI can best be seen in a dynamic context. Hence, while illuminating certain important aspects of FDI, these models are not entirely satisfactory. Finally, there is very little empirical work relating trade and investment in a formalized model, both due to the complexity of the relationships and because of data problems (cf. Naya and Ramstetter 1992: 44–49, 78).

According to the so-called Kojima hypothesis, there are two classes of FDI: trade-oriented and antitrade oriented (Kojima 1973, 1975, 1985; OECD 1987: 36), depending on whether the investment works in accordance with or against comparative advantage. In the former case, the general idea is to exploit location advantages of production in order to take better advantage of the international marketplace. Hence the source country is the one with a comparative disadvantage, and the investment tends to generate trade and enhance industrial restructuring in both source and host countries (Kojima 1973; Lizondo 1991).

In the case of antitrade oriented investment, the source country has the comparative advantage. The investment then tends to suppress trade and hinder adjustment toward greater efficiency. In this case the motive is often to exploit protected home markets in the host country, "market-protection rents." The pattern of FDI and its trade-creating effects are obviously, at least partly, a result of the general trade policy of potential host countries (cf. Blomström 1990: 5). A closed economy encourages investment aimed at the domestic market of the host country and will not create much trade.

## ROLE OF DEVELOPMENT ASSISTANCE

A third form of economic linkage is development aid. These resource transfers tend—if used properly—to lead to increasing both trade and investment, directly and indirectly, providing necessary infrastructure for industrialization, including FDI, and subsequent international trade. In the East and Southeast Asian case, Japan is the principal donor country; its contributions make up by far the largest part of aid to, for instance, ASEAN. The NIEs today do not receive any development assistance to speak of. Instead, they are becoming important donor countries themselves (cf. Grosser and Bridges 1990). Not very much is known about the details here, especially as "aid" can take many different forms apart from transfers over the balance of payments.

The aid issue has always been rather sensitive as far as the self-interest of donors is concerned. In fact, it is a common perception that bilateral aid, in particular, often reflects the interest of the donor more than that of the recipient. Political and security aspects are often involved besides the economic ones.

The allocation of Japanese aid has often been criticized, with the argument being that the Ministry of International Trade and Industry (MITI) makes plans for allocating development aid and FDI in a fashion that is supposed to be most beneficial to the Japanese (Wysocki 1990; Guisinger 1991; Hellmann 1995; cf. also Kojima 1973). Construction of infrastructure in particular is a field where the procurement process is likely to be influenced by aid donors.

The significance of this aspect is underlined by the fact that Japan today, on the one hand, is the number one donor country (World Bank, *World Development Report* 1991: 240), with about one-fifth of the total aid from the OECD, and, on the other hand, that most of its development assistant goes to Asian countries (about 60 percent at the last turn of the decade), a fact that seems to be used as "evidence" for Japan's alleged tendency to enhance its own position in the region. Additionally, while not officially part of the Japanese aid system, the Asian Development Bank (ADB) is widely regarded as "an arm of Japanese foreign policy" (Hellmann 1995).

## CONCLUSIONS AND OVERVIEW

Even without a great deal of organization, the economies of Pacific Asia seem to become more and more intertwined with Japan as the natural, albeit somewhat reluctant, center point because of its size and because all other countries in the region are still dependent on Japanese technology and capital goods. This notwithstanding, China, as an emerging market with enormous potential, appears to have taken over much of the role of the engine of growth in the region. This is the case with ASEAN, too, which, although smaller than China, grows very fast as well and is at a much higher level of development.

All this will probably lead to more organized cooperation in the future, not least because greater interdependence implies greater sensitivity in one country to what is going on in other countries in the region. Perceived needs to reconcile economic policies in the region will thus emerge. In fact, the intensity with which government and nongovernment cooperative initiatives have been put forth in the region lately may well be a symptom of just that. A huge trade potential may also still be unutilized due to trade barriers that remain despite a generally outward-looking approach of the Asia-Pacific countries.

Discussions on possible models for formalizing the trade relationships in East Asia have been quite intense during the last few years. The tendency to form trade blocs discernible in the rest of the world, threatening to leave the region outside, has been an important impetus for such discussions. The situation has calmed down, however, with the recent finalizing of the Uruguay Round of the General Agreement on Tariffs and Trade (GATT), setting the scene for further nondiscriminatory liberalizing of world trade.

If unprovoked it is likely that the Asia-Pacific countries prefer arrangements that do not aggravate relations with the United States or the European Union. The Asia-Pacific countries have so far been distinctly committed to a global trade liberalization process rather than to regional endeavors. The reason for this is certainly that the very economic success of these countries has been crucially dependent on a system of reasonably free international trade. The reluctance to exclude the United States from any formal arrangement is only partly economic: the United States is still a crucial market for the region, as well as a source for FDI, although its importance has diminished in both respects during the last few years. The other important reason is the perceived role of the United States, in a security context, as a stabilizing factor in the region.

This chapter has dealt only with the broad aggregate developments in economic interdependence in the Asia-Pacific region. To attain a more profound understanding of the processes that are effective in the region, much more research would be called for. Specifically, to be able to assess the interaction via trade, development assistance, and foreign direct investment, what is required is more detailed industrial breakdown of the figures and more research at the enterprise level. While the availability of suitable statistical data is a problem here, certainly much can still be done. Some modest results in this vein are presented in the subsequent chapters, although the main approach of this book is macroeconomic.

The plan for the rest of this book is as follows. Chapter 2 outlines a simple theory of economic development with Asian origin, the so-called "Flying Geese" model. This framework is dynamic, and although simple, it deals with the interplay between foreign trade and FDI. Much of the material presented later in the book is interpreted with the aid of this model. Chapter 3 describes the intraregional trade flows, with regard to their absolute and relative magnitude and importance over time as well as their structure, while chapter 4 employs an econometric model to assess the determinants of these flows. In chapter 5 intraregional foreign direct investment is scrutinized. In that context intraregional aid flows are discussed as well. Chapter 6 focuses on organized economic cooperation in the region, starting out from some theoretical observations, and chapter 7 looks into the oldest surviving economic organization in the region— ASEAN—in order to assess its achievements in the past and to evaluate its future prospects. Chapter 8 concludes and looks into the future.

**NOTES**

1. The term was minted in the 1970s, and although the Asian NIEs have since surpassed many OECD countries on most indicators of development, the label has stuck. I will therefore use it in this book as well, for practical reasons, in order to identify a group of countries below Japan in development, but clearly above all other Asian countries.

2. Throughout this book "Korea" refers to the Republic of Korea ("South Korea").

3. According to some economic folklore there is a "yen bloc" dominated by Japan already.

## 2

# The "Flying Geese" Model of Regional Development

## INTRODUCTION

The "Flying Geese" model is an attempt to describe the interactive development of a group of countries at different levels of industrialization, using the graphic analogy of changing patterns of leadership in a flock of flying geese. In established economic theory there are models for dealing with commodity trade, international capital flows in general, and foreign direct investment. Some theoretical frameworks, such as the so-called dependency theory, also try to address the economic relations between countries at a more general level. Most of these theories are difficult to take full advantage of at the macroeconomic level, partly because they are usually hard to unite in one coherent framework that is not too complicated to be practical, and partly because some of the more comprehensive frameworks have been criticized for being tautological and ideologically biased. Although not free from problems, the analytical framework presented here, the "Flying Geese" model, incorporating both trade and FDI, appears to be a useful tool for dealing with regional economic interaction between a group of countries, especially when these are at different levels of development. It is also useful for understanding the industrial policy, and arguably foreign aid policy, pursued in Japan and in East Asia in general.

The concept of the "Flying Geese" goes back to the time before World War II, but has been little known by Western economists until recently. In Japan, however, this theory is common knowledge among economists. The reason for the recent interest in the model by Western economists is no doubt the rapid ascendance of several East Asian countries to a status of important industrial producers and actors in international trade. As this development is frequently seen as a "miracle," scholars have been keen to look for explanations, even unconventional ones, for what is going on in this region.

The "Flying Geese" model was originally constructed as a piece of applied economics only. Nevertheless, its flavor of political economy is very clear. In the background there was always the interest of the Japanese nation in the international context, and the "Flying Geese" helped to interpret the regional activities of Japan in a positive, almost altruistic fashion (cf. Korhonen 1992: 186). Such an approach was useful after the war, both in the rhetoric of domestic politics and in the contacts with the country's Asian neighbors. Due to their experiences before and during World War II, the latter, as well as many scholars, were often suspicious, however, and tended to see the model as a rationalization of economic, and perhaps political, imperialism. This attitude has survived, to some extent, until this day.

The foundation of the "Flying Geese" framework was laid in the early and mid-1930s by the late Professor Kaname Akamatsu. Akamatsu was familiar with Marxist-Hegelian thinking and saw economic development as a kind of dialectic, deterministic, and unstoppable process, gradually taking an economy to higher levels of sophistication. The original focus of the model was on Japan only. The model seems to have been one of the rationales lending legitimacy to the expansion of the Japanese presence in the region before and during World War II (see Holden 1991 and Korhonen 1994). After the war, the theory envisaged a way for Japan to catch up with the Western industrialized countries (Korhonen 1994). The application to the case of regional economic interdependence in general emerged only gradually. As an analytical framework, there is now nothing in the model that limits its possible applications to Japan and its neighbors.

The ideas of Akamatsu were virtually unknown in the West until he published his model, in a more developed form, in two articles in English in the early 1960s (Akamatsu 1961, 1962). In Japan, he was remarkably influential during the whole postwar period, and his ideas were guidelines for those responsible for the Japanese industrial reconstruction after the war (Korhonen 1992: 68). The late international dissemination of the "Flying Geese" model may—apart from the language problem—have been due to its role as an economic-theoretical underpinning of the Japanese expansionary policy before and during the war, which, of course, did nothing to alleviate the suspicions against the model mentioned above. After the war, Japan was occupied and virtually cut off from mainland Asia by this and other circumstances. Although the model was never abandoned in Japan, and was often referred to in the Japanese literature, it did not turn up much until the 1970s in the internationally published writings of Japanese economists. The best known of these are Kiyoshi Kojima, who elaborated especially the role of FDI, and Terutomo Ozawa, who has tried to generalize the theory beyond the relation between Japan and its neighboring countries. Lee (e.g., 1990) has made important contributions as well, clarifying the relations between structural change, trade, and FDI.

Former foreign minister and academic Saburo Okita seems to have been the person who more than anyone conveyed the concept to a more general public, in the late 1970s (Cronin 1992: 28), although the somewhat related idea of forming a Pacific free trade area was mooted as early as 1965 by Kojima, an idea taken up by the then foreign minister of Japan, Takeo Miki (Korhonen 1992: 9–10). Today the framework is well known and widely used among students of East Asia, even though the attitude of many economists is still lukewarm.

Apart from the possible descriptive "correctness" of the model, it has been regarded as useful for understanding the Japanese industrial policy and the way the Japanese interpret their international environment (cf., e.g., Rapp 1975). This double role, as both a description and—in a way—a prescription, is important to understand.

The "Flying Geese" model is not a watertight theoretical construction in the sense that it can be deduced formally from a given set of assumptions, nor is it one alternative for explaining economic development in an open economy context that can be tested against other, competing models. Rather it is an inductive type of model, to a great extent induced from the Japanese experience of industrialization. It consists of a set of related, rather loosely formulated ideas—if modern economic theory is used as the yardstick—on structural change and economic interdependence between open economies, where different elements are often perfectly compatible with mainstream economic analysis. Moreover, the model has been formulated as three different, although interrelated varieties. First, it can be used to visualise the development over time of one industry only. Second, if we observe several industries at a time, it can illuminate the change in the industrial structure in one country; and third, it can be employed to show the interdependence between different countries as foreign trade is affected by the rise and fall of industries and of transfers of productive resources between countries.

The specific purpose of this chapter is to present the essence of the "Flying Geese" model, both from a descriptive and a political economy point of view, and to discuss the implications of the model on trade, industrial, and foreign aid policy issues. The purpose here is not to interpret recent developments in the Asia-Pacific region in terms of the model—a theme taken up in subsequent chapters—or to discuss how it possibly could be amended to keep up with a changing reality. The latter issue would be a worthwhile object for further research, however.

## THE DYNAMICS OF TRADE FLOWS AND PRODUCTION STRUCTURE

Akamatsu focused on a group of countries developing together in two main groups, the "leaders" and the "followers" (and possibly some in between) but with a common "goal" in the form of ever higher levels of technological sophistication (cf. Korhonen 1992: 69). The relative position of countries on the ladder of development does not necessarily stay unchanged, however, but some followers may move faster than others and gradually advance toward the leading position, while earlier leaders may lose momentum after some time and may be overtaken by other countries. The configuration of countries and its development over time are thus similar to a flock of flying wild geese.

Akamatsu realized that no country could hope for more than a temporary advantage over others. Permanent domination of some countries over others is not possible with this type of development pattern. As a matter of fact, the position of a "follower" country is easier than that of a leader, as the latter has to make continuous efforts in order to remain at the technological edge. Hence it is not possible to create a stable international division of labor (Korhonen 1994, 1992: 76, 78).

Originally, the "Flying Geese" refers to the microeconomic pattern of development, however, sometimes referred to as the catching-up product cycle (Yamazawa 1990) of one industry, as illustrated in Figure 2.1. In the figure, panel A illustrates the hypothetical behavior of domestic production, domestic demand, exports, and imports of a particular product. Panel B illustrates the behavior of imports and exports as shares of domestic demand and production, respectively; and in panel C, finally, the relation between domestic production and domestic demand is depicted. The horizontal axis measures the time dimension and is divided into five stages of development: introductory, import substitution, export, mature, and reverse import.

In the first stage, domestic demand develops, presumably because of information from abroad on the availability of a product and subsequent imports. The imports of cheap foreign goods drive craftsmen out of work and disrupt the stationary state of a less developed country, but simultaneously bring forth the labor force necessary for future industrial expansion.

Availability of the product tends to change the habits of the population, and as the demand increases, domestic production is taken up, in a second stage, through technology transfer or imitation, but cannot replace entirely the imported product due to a low quality/price ratio of the domestic product. In the next stage, import substitution takes place because of learning effects, standardized technologies, and larger volumes allowing economies of scale to be taken advantage of.[1] The relative production costs, as compared to more advanced countries, tend to be low, and thus the production is competitive, also internationally. In the third, export stage, the domestic production spills over into exports, and while the domestic demand gradually stops growing, the momentum of production can be kept up by increasing exports. (The above three stages constitute the original form of the model; cf. also Korhonen 1994 and 1992: 73.)

In the mature (fourth) stage, domestic demand stagnates or decreases and exports decline, the latter because production has now been taken up by other, less developed countries with lower production costs, and because the growth of demand of the product itself slows down at the global level. In the final, fifth stage there will be net imports again, even if domestic production may not disappear altogether, when the domestic producers are outcompeted by foreign firms (including overseas subsidiaries of domestic firms). Meanwhile, other industries producing more advanced manufactures and in particular, capital goods needed to produce the consumer goods being produced already, enter the import-substituting and export stages, as the comparative advantages of the country change. Hence the industrial structure changes over time according to dynamic comparative advantages. Note that the country under consideration may import both more and less capital intensive goods than what its own production range consists of (to see this, see the theoretical exposition of Krueger 1977).

This part of the story is, of course, entirely compatible with mainstream neoclassical economics, according to which the pattern of specialization in production and trade changes with changes in relative factor endowments (i.e., comparative advantages), as discussed in detail in the Appendix, although

Akamatsu did not argue in terms of comparative advantages. It should be noted, however, that due to technological progress, different industries may display different factor proportions at different times. The use of robots, for example, may transform a labor-intensive industry to a technology-intensive one, as some examples from the garment industry demonstrate (Blomström 1994). This is then another reason for structural change, apart from changing factor endowments.

Traditional theory assumes that there is no mobility of factors of production across national borders, however. In the "Flying Geese" framework, physical, financial and human capital[2] from the declining industries can be used for FDI (Akamatsu 1962). (Labor, especially unskilled labor, on the other hand, is much more immobile across national borders.) In this way FDI contributes to structural changes in the less developed host countries as well. Of course, it is conceivable that the obsolete factors simply could be sold to less developed countries. The problem is that factors of production are, although mobile, sometimes difficult to sell off in the short term, for example, due to the need for complementary know-how, and sometimes the firms may prefer not to sell or lease intangible technology due to the consequent lack of control and fear of abuse. Kojima's theory of FDI, which will be commented on later, can be interpreted as an attempt to capture this part of the "Flying Geese" process (cf. Peltola 1994).

**Figure 2.1**
**The Catching-Up Product Cycle**

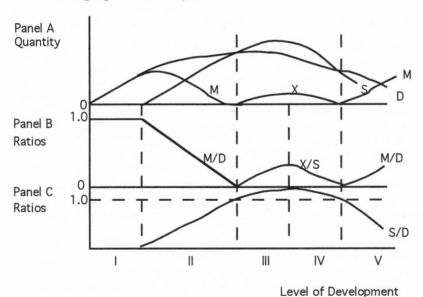

*Source:* adapted from Yamazawa 1990: 20.

At the micro level, the resemblance to the well-known product cycle theory (Vernon 1966) is striking, although the interplay between production, demand, exports, and imports is rather different.[3] Moreover, it should be stressed that Vernon based his idea on a framework of imperfect competition. The "Flying Geese" model is also fully compatible with perfect competition, as the product cycle in the latter case is driven by changing comparative advantages. As made clear by Rapp (1975), the main difference is due to the fact that for a country not at the technological frontier "new" products are usually introduced via imports, while production is taken up later on, often supported by protectionist measures.

Government intervention may change the details in the process outlined above. Especially in the early phases of the cycle, government measures, falling under the import substitution and export promotion categories, can be used to speed up different phases of the process. Because of learning effects, aggressive export promotion at an early stage of the product cycle may reduce unit costs and further enhance export penetration. In the late phase of reverse import, the government may slow down the process by imposing trade barriers or by subsidizing the domestic industry (cf. Yamazawa 1990: 32). A "Flying Geese" pattern of development may also take place through systematic changes of exchange rates, as suggested by Kwan (1994: 32–35).[4] It is no use, however, for any government to try to conserve a certain production structure, as the system tends to develop in a way that renders such attempts more and more futile. In industries where the production process is easily split up into subprocesses, such as in the consumer electronics and automotive industries, the restructuring process is often very fast.

The "Flying Geese" pattern is dynamic, while the orthodox trade models are based on comparative statics. The production structures overlap to a certain extent in different countries, as is obvious from the catching-up product cycle.[5] Hence, at a national level, the countries complement each other but also compete to some extent. The "follower" in general, as noted by Rapp (1975), can start from lower unit costs than the innovator and may thus overtake the latter just by growing faster.

The dynamics of the model are thus inherent partly in the competitive process implicitly embodied in the overlaps of two or more countries' industrial structure and, more fundamentally, in the changing relative endowments of factors of production over time. This mixture of a competitive and a complementary structure is the driving force of the "dialectic process" (Akamatsu 1961) propelling the geese formation. It should be noted that the microeconomic process in Figure 2.1 is incomplete in the sense that the driving forces behind the development over time are not fully explained. In order for the depicted process to take place, the relative endowments of the factors of production have to change (cf. Yamazawa 1990: 33).

At the macro level, the "Flying Geese" model describes the changing industrial structure in economies at different levels of development. A particular industry, according to this framework, emerges, grows and recedes in a group of economies in an order determined by the dynamic comparative advantages in each economy. The present structure of an economy holds the seeds to its own destruction and is gradually succeeded by another structure, which in turn is doomed to be destroyed in the longer run. This way of seeing the development process clearly points to the Marxist origins of Akamatsu's thinking. Depicting the development of a particular industry over time in several countries, we would end up with a series of inverted u-shaped curves, allegedly reminding one of the wings of a flock of flying geese, one for each economy (cf. Kwan 1994: 82–83).

Another way of capturing the essence of the idea of the "Flying Geese" on the macroeconomic level is depicted in Figure 2.2. In this figure, value added per employment (in industry) is used as a rough approximation of "sophistication" of the production structure in an economy. The position and length of an arrow denotes the range of goods produced in a certain economy. This proxy for sophistication is certainly highly positively correlated with GDP per capita, but, primarily because endowments of natural resources differ, the income level may differ between economies producing approximately in the same range of goods. Over time, the flock moves to the right and upwards, in the direction of the arrows. The economies involved thus tend to move in a V-formation, like a flying flock of wild geese.

Now, choose a country somewhere in the midst of the group, say, E. This economy tends to import raw materials and simple components from its less developed neighbors and more advanced capital goods and consumer durables, not domestically produced, from more advanced countries. If the stock of capital and "know-how" expands faster than that of "raw" labor, the relative factor endowments change, inducing the country gradually to abandon production of the more labor-intensive goods (which can profitably be overtaken by other, more labor-abundant countries) and take up the production of goods that require

**Figure 2.2**
**Macroeconomic   Development**

GDP/capita

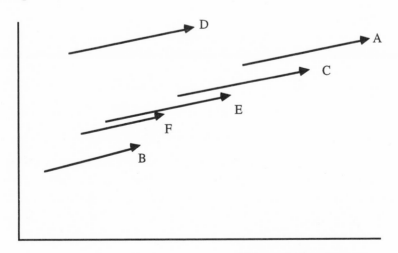

Value added/employment

more real and human capital. As the accumulation of capital continues, however, even more capital-intensive production will be taken up, and the production structure will be further upgraded. (In reality, of course, technological breakthroughs may change this pattern, in the sense that a "sunset" industry may be revived and make a comeback in a country from which it has been disappearing already.)

The level of development of a country can be determined, within a "Flying Geese" framework, by the foreign trade structure using a specialization index.[6] In Figure 2.3 below, which follows Kwan (1994: 84–85), the development of such an index is followed up in three sectors: primary goods (SITC 0–4, and 68), "other" manufactures (SITC 5, 6, 8, and 9, excluding 68), and machinery (SITC 7). The idea is that in each country the primary sector develops first, then "other" manufacturing, and last the machinery industry, which is the most advanced sector in terms of technology and human capital intensity.

Hence the position of each country in a development continuum can be determined by the relative value of the specialization index for the different industries. Kwan (1994: 85) suggests the classification presented in Table 2.1. The stages are: Developing Country, Young Newly Industrializing Economy (NIE), Mature NIE, and Industrialized Country.[7]

**Figure 2.3**
**Changes in Trade Specialization over Time**

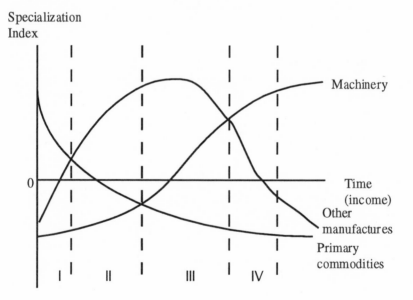

*Source*: adapted from Kwan 1994: 85.

**Table 2.1**
**Relative Values of the Specialization Index for Different Stages of Development**

*Specialization index for*

| | | | |
|---|---|---|---|
| I. Developing country stage | Primary commodities > | Other manufactures > | Machinery |
| II. Young NIE stage | Other manufactures > | Primary commodities > | Machinery |
| III. Mature NIE stage | Other manufactures > | Machinery > | Primary commodities |
| IV. Industrialized country stage | Machinery > | Other manufactures > | Primary commodities |

*Source*: Kwan 1994: 85.

## THE ROLE OF FOREIGN DIRECT INVESTMENT

Not too long ago, FDI was looked upon with suspicion in both developed and developing countries. Not only was the sociopolitical influence of foreigners unpopular, but the foreign firms were frequently considered a threat to domestic industry. This attitude did have some justification in the era of import-substituting industrialization. This strategy tends to foster overprotected and inefficient domestic firms with little resistance to offer to intruding foreign firms, usually branches of multinational enterprises with the best available technologies at their command. In an open trade regime, the industrial structure of a country tends to be much more in line with the actual comparative advantages of its economy, and hence the domestic firms tend to be much more resilient.

Although not much discussed in the original versions of the "Flying Geese" model—the scope for FDI in the 1930s was limited at best—international direct investment is easily fitted into this framework. Inward investment may help the catch-up process in a developing country to get started, especially as FDI is basically a "package deal" bringing in industry-specific know-how, including management, marketing, and especially international market access. Outward investment, in turn, becomes interesting for declining industries, which may survive by moving their production process, or part of it, abroad.

As pointed out by several authors, for example, Kojima and Ozawa (1984) and Phongpaichit (1990: 5), the Japanese approach to FDI, represented above all by Kojima (e.g., 1973, 1975, 1985), differs in an interesting way from that of mainstream economics. While the latter developed the theory from a microeconomic point of view (for a succinct survey, see Lizondo 1991), focusing on the behavior of the multinational corporation, the Japanese approach was concentrated on (changing) comparative advantage, to which firms adapt through, for example, engaging themselves in FDI. These theoretical elements, rather than contradicting each other, are mostly complementary, however, although the Japanese approach has been severely criticized for ignoring crucial aspects of microeconomics. Kojima has developed his theory over the years as a response to criticism from mainstream researchers on multinational corporations but has not, by and large, been able to fend away the criticism (cf., e.g., Buckley 1985, 1991). Since these later developments do not relate much to the "Flying Geese" model, they are not dealt with here.

According to the so-called Kojima hypothesis, there are two classes of FDI: trade-oriented and antitrade-oriented (Kojima 1973, 1975, 1985; OECD 1987: 36), depending on whether the investment works in harmony with or against comparative advantage. In the former case, the general idea is to exploit location advantages of production in order to take better advantage of the international marketplace. Hence the source country is the one with a comparative disadvantage, and the investment tends to generate trade and enhance industrial restructuring in both source and host countries as the share of industries with a comparative advantage (or at least a potential comparative advantage) grows, compared to other industries (Daquila and Nguyen 1994; Kojima 1973; Lizondo 1991; Mortimore 1993).

Investments in low-tech industries may also be beneficial in the sense that the technology is easier for the host country to adopt, which may facilitate linkage effects through subcontracting in the host country. Since the investments in this case do not represent frontline technology, the investors are often willing to cooperate in joint ventures with domestic firms (Ozawa 1979: 72–75; Blomström 1994).

In the latter (that is, antitrade-oriented) case, the FDI is in industries where the investor has a comparative advantage. The investor wants to protect his oligopolistic advantage, and a crucial objective is preserving the investor's market share (Peltola 1994). This type of investment will substitute domestic production for trade, and in the process is likely to drive the domestic firms of the host country out of business. Moreover, being technologically superior, this type of investment can link up to a very limited extent with domestic firms in the host economy. Kojima's hypothesis was that Japanese investment is predominantly of the former type, while American investment is allegedly of the latter type. As the "American" investment pattern does not comply with comparative advantage, Kojima concludes that it tends to reduce welfare in both source and host countries. (The welfare effects of different types of FDI are discussed by Kojima and Ozawa 1984.)

Kojima's ideas have been formalized by Kojima and Ozawa (1984, 1985). The scope for international trade is created by a situation with internationally immobile factors of production and mobile goods. (If capital is mobile, the relative capital/labor abundance, and hence the relative price of labor and capital, are equalized. In that case, no foundation for [traditional] trade remains.) Kojima and Ozawa want to show that a third factor of production, mobile industry-specific "entrepreneurial endowment," [8] may render trade more advantageous than in the traditional Heckscher-Ohlin case, if the other factors are immobile and if there are differences in the relative stock of that third factor between the industries.

Even without specific "entrepreneurial endowment," an industry with a comparative disadvantage could improve its profitability by relocating to a country where the same industry has a comparative advantage (cf. Lee 1990). The FDI in this case comprises the firm-specific corporate assets (e.g., technology and management skills). This reallocation of resources tends to widen the basis for trade and enhance welfare in both source and host countries.

In a less restrictive context, where capital is mobile in addition to know-how, outward FDI may be useful in industries that are losing their previous comparative advantage in the home country. Since capital is homogeneous only in abstract neoclassical models, in reality it cannot generally be transferred to the growing sectors of the economy. Instead, the firms may use the fact that other countries still have comparative advantages similar to those of the home country at an earlier stage, and make an FDI to the latter countries instead of closing down (cf. Lee 1990). In such a way, the firm can utilize its capital and know-how, while the production capacity of the host country is increased (cf. Yamazawa 1990: 35–36 and Jesudason 1989: 177, 183).

Kojima's hypothesis has not, by and large, stood the test of time very well in the sense that distinct types of investment cannot readily be discerned for different source countries, even if his thesis is still subject to debate.[9] This is the fact especially for more recent years (cf., e.g., Chou 1988; Hill 1990; see also, e.g., Ariff 1991: 123). This does not mean, however, that Kojima's idea in itself has become irrelevant. What it does mean is apparently that the type of FDI cannot easily be classified according to source country.[10] Indeed it would be rather surprising if this were possible. Kojima's theory is not very useful for explaining FDI between countries at a similar level of development, where differences in relative factor abundance is usually small. It is not difficult to think of other cases, either, where this theory seems less well suited. For instance, high-tech investments in developing countries may sometimes make perfect sense from both a private and a social point of view. This is when the host country is able to participate in the development of the product, besides functioning as a market. India as a base for software development is a case in point. Hence Kojima's ideas can hardly be interpreted as a general theory of FDI (cf. Peltola 1994).

## THE ROLE OF DEVELOPMENT AID

A third form of economic linkage, relevant for regional interdependence, is development aid. Such resource transfers may lead to increasing trade both directly and indirectly, providing necessary infrastructure for industrialization and subsequent international trade. In the case of East Asia, Japan is now the principal donor whose contributions make up the bulk of development assistance in ASEAN. The NIEs today do not receive any aid to speak of, although Korea and Taiwan did so during an earler phase of their development.

Aid does not have any specific role in the original formulations of the "Flying Geese" model. If the model is conceived as an economic policy guideline, however, development aid may be planned in order to facilitate a regional and international restructuring of industry. The allocation of Japanese aid has often been discussed critically, arguing that the Ministry of International Trade and Industry makes plans for allocating development aid and FDI in a fashion that is supposed to be most beneficial to the Japanese. This issue is discussed in somewhat more detail in Chapter 5.

## CONCLUSIONS

The preceding discussion takes us directly to the issue of the ideological significance and policy influence of the "Flying Geese" model. It must be stressed again that the model originally did not contain strong normative elements, at least not explicitly, such as suggestions concerning industrial policy, regional integration, or political cooperation. Despite this, the theory seems to have had a strong influence on the thinking of Japanese policymakers through its general influence on their way of perceiving the economic realities. As pointed out by Korhonen (1992: 76), "its importance . . . lies in its way of understanding the global economic system, and Japan's place in it."

In Japan, industrial policy has always been active, with an aim toward discarding comparatively disadvantaged industries and favoring comparatively advantaged ones (cf. Kojima and Ozawa 1984; Tran 1988). Gradually the ideas propounded by the model have spread among scholars in other countries as well. The deterministic nature of the model may also have contributed to the general feeling of development optimism that can be discerned so clearly in East Asia. The implicit message, implying that as economic prosperity spreads, no country can hope for dominating the global economy in the long term, has probably been important, too (cf. Korhonen 1992: 77). In this context we may draw the reader's attention to the fact that industrial restructuring today reflects the decisions of a relatively small number of MNCs apart from policy measures proper, taken by governments. This may add to the determinism as understood from the point of view of national governments.

In a way the "Flying Geese" model is significant regardless of whether it is "correct" or not, judged as an economic-theoretical model. Although formally a purely economic-theoretical framework, the "Flying Geese" model evidently has a hidden agenda which guides and directs the economic policy both toward the domestic industries and toward other regional economies. The model can easily be seen as a prescription, founded on the historical development of Japan, determining both a goal for the development process and the means to be used (Korhonen 1994). The conscious policy of industrial upgrading that has been taking place in many East Asian countries (see, e.g., for the case of Singapore, *Straits Times*, August 12, 1995), followed by foreign direct investments by the same countries in other regional economies, seems to fit into this framework extremely well.

The "Flying Geese" model is an interesting attempt to capture a dynamic process of international interdependence, despite deficiencies and the fact that it is not necessarily a panacea for a developing open economy. The model is formally about economics alone, if interpreted strictly, without explicit political connotations. As already noted, such political and policy implications are not very deep beneath the surface, however. Ideas about Japan's role in the regional context, the changes in these ideas over time, and the implications for industrial policy implicit in the model are the most obvious examples.

Possible parallels regarding the political interdependence between nations could also be drawn (Korhonen 1994). In that case, too, permanent domination by the leading countries is doomed to fail. Nevertheless, those countries may well try to exert their influence to their less powerful neighbors by military force or by divide-and-rule politics. Their efforts will be marred by a process similar to the one at work in the realm of industrial development. Foreign influence will cause domestic cultural and political institutions to crumble, but the more a country is influenced by foreign impulses at an early stage—which tends to be the case when the degree of domination is great—the less dependent it will become in the future.

In the field of international trade and FDI, reality has been changing rapidly during the last few decades. Indeed theory has not always been able to develop at the same pace. As for the "Flying Geese," the theory is not very rigorous, as has become clear above. Hence it can accommodate most of the main lines of development without too many difficulties. Much should be done to refine the framework, however. Issues like the effect of changing exchange rates, shortening product cycles, the emergence of subregional economic zones, "growth triangles," and the danger of "hollowing out" in more advanced countries are only a few example of issues that should be addressed within the framework of the model. In spite of the need for more elaboration of details, it is important to do so in a way that does not sacrifice the general overview provided by the "Flying Geese" model.

## APPENDIX: NEOCLASSICAL TRADE THEORY AND THE "FLYING GEESE"

In order to analyze the ideas on restructuring of trade and production, within the more formalized framework of the neoclassical model for international trade, it is helpful to generalize the standard 2 x 2 model into an n x m model, that is, a model with m countries and n products. We retain, for expositional simplicity, the assumption of two factors of production. The basic structure of our model is based on Krueger (1977).

We assume, as usual in this context, identical technologies in all countries, constant returns to scale, and strictly quasi-concave production functions. We also assume that there are no factor-intensity reversals (that is, if the products are ordered according to their labor intensity, the ordering is always the same, irrespective of the wage-capital cost ratio). This implies that this ordering of products, according to factor intensity, is identical in all countries, no matter what the goods prices are. We assume, moreover, that the international product price ratios are exogenously given and that consumer preferences are given and identical in all countries. (The latter assumption does not, of course, affect production patterns, but it does affect trade patterns.)

Now, with full factor mobility *within* an economy, and no mobility *between* countries, each country will produce at a point where the common wage-capital cost ratio is equal to the ratio of the marginal products of labor and capital, respectively. Thus each country operates on its production possibility frontier, at a point where the goods price ratios are equal to the corresponding marginal rate of transformation (marginal opportunity cost ratio).

In the standard Heckscher-Ohlin model, the only difference between countries is their relative factor endowments. Assume for the moment that these are given and constant. Countries can now be ordered according to their relative abundance of, say, labor. The abundance, in its turn, determines the shape of their production possibility frontiers, according to Rybczynski's theorem (see, e.g., Södersten and Reed 1994: 125–127). Figure A2.1 illustrates the reasoning for the two-product, two-country case. We assume that A is the relatively capital-abundant country, and that X is the labor-intensive good, and Y the capital-intensive one. In that case the production possibility curves look like the ones in Figure A2.1. (AA and BB are the production possibility curves for A and B, respectively.)

Assume that the international price ratio, $p_X/p_Y$, is given as pp. As the figure is drawn, both countries produce some of both goods, although country A is quite specialized on product Y and country B on product X. If the price ratio is low (high) enough, both countries specialize on Y (X) only, the required ratio

**Figure A2.1**
**Production Structures with Different Factor Endowments**

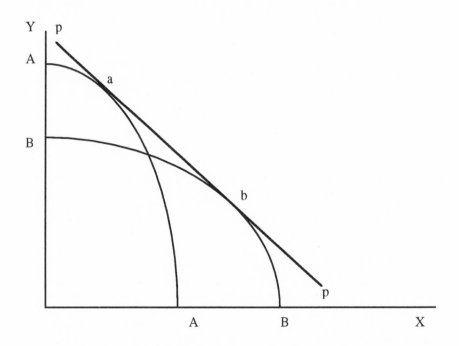

having to be lower in the case of B than in the case of A to induce complete specialization in Y and vice versa. If we start with complete specialization on Y, increasing the quantity of labor available changes the shape of the production possibility curve, lowering its slope at any combination of X and Y. In the context of Figure A2.1, a country can thus either produce one product (in which case the wage-capital cost ratio is determined by the production function for that product only) or two products, which gives the wage-capital cost ratio as a function of the (given) price ratio. Changing relative factor endowments thus change the optimal production structure, which, with given consumer preferences, changes the optimal trade pattern as well.

With more than two products, it can be shown (Krueger 1977: 4) that the exact product composition is indeterminate, while the factor price ratio is determined by the price ratio of any two products. A possible production structure in the n x m case is shown in Figure A2.2. The products are ordered from the most to the least labor intensive, while the countries are ordered from the most to the least labor abundant. An overlap in product ranges is, of course, always possible (as in the "Flying Geese" case), but a country farther "down the line" can never produce a good more labor intensive that the ones produced by the preceding country. In Figure A2.2 there is one additional important point to be noted: although the production pattern is given by the figure, the trade pattern is still indeterminate, since the latter is of course determined jointly with the (implicit) demand side in the model. Thus we cannot know, a priori, whether a certain commodity will be an import-competing or an export product. In a dynamic setting, as we will see below, it is, however, possible to study the transformation of the status of a product, for example, from a nonproduced product to an import-competing one and further to an export product.

In dynamizing the above production pattern we can simulate a behavior very similar to the "Flying Geese" hypothesis. A changing pattern can be brought about either by letting the relative commodity prices change continuously in a certain direction, or letting the relative factor endowments change over time. Since capital accumulation (physical and human) is a central feature of the "Flying Geese" model, and since we chose to work with exogenous relative product prices in the above model, the latter alternative seems most natural. For simplicity, we assume that changes in the factor endowment ratio take place only in one country. We start from the assumption that a labor-abundant country starts accumulating capital at a faster rate than the rate of growth of its labor force, keeping the relative product prices and factor proportions in all other countries constant. According to Rybczynski's theorem, mentioned above, this will lead to a change in the optimal product composition toward the more capital-intensive goods. Obviously, if we start out from a situation where only one, labor-intensive product were produced and let the capital stock start increasing, at some stage the economy would take up the production of the "next" (in terms of Figure A2.2 ), slightly more capital-intensive commodity, followed by the next in order, and so on. At the starting point the country would be an importer of all products except for the most labor-intensive one. When a new product is taken up, it starts as an import-substituting commodity, gradually covering more and more of the domestic demand, and finally becoming an export product. At some stage the most labor-intensive product is left out of the product line, followed by the second most labor intensive, and so forth. All countries, except the two extremes, import both more capital-intensive and more labor-intensive goods than they produce themselves, a trade pattern that is strikingly similar to that of the "Flying Geese" model. Obviously our story here is, as a whole, similar to the latter one. In Figure A2.2, this process implies that the country considered is moving down and to the right.

An interesting by-product of the above dynamization of the neoclassical model is the fact that it clearly demonstrates the irrelevance of sorts of the distinction between import substitution and export orientation in the absence of price distortions. Import substitution is not *by nature* inferior to export orientation, a fact not always well understood in the literature on trade and industrialization strategies (cf. Bulmer-Thomas 1988: 105–117; Singer and Alizadeh 1986; and Arndt 1990 for illuminating discussions of this point, which is too far-reaching to be discussed within this Appendix). What matters is whether the production structure complies with the comparative advantages of an economy or not. Whether a product will be exported or not depends on prevailing demand conditions. In reality, of course, import substitution has usually been pursued with the aid of severely distorting policies, which will be discussed in more detail in Chapter 3.

**Figure A2.2**
**Example of Production Patterns in a Ten-Country, Ten-Product Case**

Product, in Order of Labor Intensity

Country, in Order of Labor Abundance

|    | 1 | 2 | 3 | 4 | 5 | 6 | 7 | 8 | 9 | 10 |
|----|---|---|---|---|---|---|---|---|---|----|
| 1  | X |   |   |   |   |   |   |   |   |    |
| 2  |   | X | X | X |   |   |   |   |   |    |
| 3  |   |   | X | X | X |   |   |   |   |    |
| 4  |   |   |   | X | X |   |   |   |   |    |
| 5  |   |   |   |   | X | X | X |   |   |    |
| 6  |   |   |   |   |   | X | X |   |   |    |
| 7  |   |   |   |   |   |   | X | X |   |    |
| 8  |   |   |   |   |   |   |   | X | X |    |
| 9  |   |   |   |   |   |   |   |   | X | X  |
| 10 |   |   |   |   |   |   |   |   |   | X  |

*Source:* adapted from Krueger 1977: 7.

## NOTES

1. As the present model illustrates well, "import substitution" and "export orientation" are not different strategies in themselves but rather different phases in a product cycle. The terms, when used to denote trade policies at a macroeconomic level, are different in the sense that they refer to systematic discrimination of imports versus domestically produced goods, or exports versus domestically sold products, respectively.

2. Production, management and marketing know-how.

3. The "original" (in fact, of course, the "Flying Geese" paradigm is much older) product cycle involves the invention and pilot launching stages of the product which is much more demanding than just commencing production of an already existing product (cf. Kojima 1977: 154). The product cycle theory focuses on the development of a new product and concentrates on the production process, given factor endowments. Moreover the latter theory is more concerned with the source country in the context of FDI, whereas the "Flying Geese" is more concerned with the host country.

4. As the exchange rate of the yen surged after the so-called Plaza Accord in 1985 the Asian NIEs could expand their exports to a considerable extent (especially to the US), partly with the aid of Japanese FDI. As a result, the exchange rate of the NIEs rose in turn which encouraged a capital outflow to other Asian countries, in particular ASEAN and China. The exports of the latter then started to increase.

5. There are certainly other reasons for overlapping production structures, too, e.g. in the form of other determinants of competitive advantage as explained by e.g. Michael Porter (1990: 11–21). Moreover, some industries are regarded as more "strategic" than others e.g. because of external effects they may generate for the benefit of the rest of the economy (cf. e.g. Krugman 1986). Such industries may be kept going with the aid of subsidies etc. even if they are not profitable as such. Still, however "strategic" an activity is considered, it can only be pursued by an economy with a minimum of physical and human capital endowments.

6. $SI_i = (X_i - M_i)/(X_i + M_i)$, where $X_i$ and $M_i$ are the exports and imports in industry i. The index goes from -1 to +1, a higher value representing a higher degree of specialisation (or "international competitiveness").

7. This way of classifying economies seems to make sense, by and large, even if it is not completely unproblematic. In particular, very resource-rich countries like Australia and some oil exporters of the Middle East have trade structures that fall in the "developing country" category despite their high income level. Similarly, resource-poor countries, like Singapore, may export large quantities of primary products at an earlier stage of development, but then the products come, of course, from trading and not from domestic sources.

8. This entrepreneurial endowment is rather firm-specific than industry-specific. However, as explained by Porter (1990) this type of endowment tends to be clustered in some industries rather than in others.

9. For instance, Mortimore (1993) finds clear differences between American investment in Latin America and Japanese investment in Asia.

10. The pattern of FDI and its trade-creating effects are obviously, at least partly, a result of the general trade policy of potential host countries (cf. Blomström 1990: 5).

# 3

## Intraregional Trade and Specialization Patterns in East Asia

### INTRODUCTION

Asia is the region that has experienced the most rapid growth of international (merchandise) trade during recent years. In 1970, only 12 percent of world exports came from East Asia, while the corresponding figures for 1982 and 1993 were 17 and 26 percent respectively. For imports, the share of the region was 13, 16, and 23 percent, respectively (International Monetary Fund; various issues, Government of the Republic of China, *Statistical Yearbook of the Republic of China*, various issues). Much of the increase is, in fact, intraregional trade. Intraregional trade grew by an average of 10.5 percent during the 1980s, for instance (Lloyd 1994). Some authors (cf. Cronin 1992: 9) conclude that the Asia-Pacific region has now reached the critical mass for self-sustained growth. Despite this, the continuing importance of the North American and European markets should not be underestimated. In Table 3.1 the world trade shares of the East Asian economies in 1982 and 1993 are shown.

The interdependence between the East Asian economies in terms of trade and investment has only recently attracted the attention of researchers (cf., e.g., Kwan 1994; World Bank 1994). The fact is, however, that in many respects this interdependence was still stronger in the prewar period. In 1938, 67 percent of the trade of East Asia was intraregional, which is much more than today (World Bank 1994: 21). Interdependence cannot be measured by trade shares only, however. Much of the early trade within the region must have been exchange of rather unprocessed commodities through the major regional entrepôts, Hong Kong, Manila, Shanghai, and Singapore. Although important, this trade is not necessarily a reliable sign of a high degree of de facto integration between the East Asian economies. With the exception of Japan and a few small pockets of industrial and trading activity, all of these were backward and rural at that time. Moreover, the strong presence of colonial powers in the region certainly contributed to forming the trade patterns.

Table 3.1
Global Trade Shares of the East Asian Countries, 1982 and 1993
(percentages)

| | Exports | | Imports | |
|---|---|---|---|---|
| | 1982 | 1993 | 1982 | 1993 |
| Japan | 8.1 | 9.8 | 7.3 | 6.4 |
| Korea | 1.3 | 2.3 | 1.4 | 2.2 |
| Hong Kong | 1.2 | 3.7 | 1.3 | 3.7 |
| Taiwan | 1.3 | 2.3 | 1.1 | 2.1 |
| China | 1.3 | 2.5 | 1.1 | 2.8 |
| Vietnam | — | 0.1 | — | 0.1 |
| Brunei | 0.2 | 0.1 | — | 0.1 |
| Indonesia | 1.3 | 1.0 | 0.9 | 0.8 |
| Malaysia | 0.7 | 1.3 | 0.7 | 1.2 |
| Philippines | 0.3 | 0.3 | 0.5 | 0.5 |
| Singapore | 1.2 | 2.0 | 1.6 | 2.3 |
| Thailand | 0.4 | 1.0 | 0.5 | 1.2 |
| East Asia* | 17.4 | 26.3 | 16.3 | 23.3 |

* Includes the listed countries only.
*Source:* Compiled from International Monetary Fund, *Directions of Trade Statistics,* various issues;
        Government of the Republic of China, *Statistical Yearbook of the Republic of China,* 1990.

After the war, the importance of intra-East Asian trade diminished drastically, mainly due to the poor state of the region's economies at the time. After this, the trans-Pacific trade picked up first, while the share of intraregional trade began to increase from the 1970s on (World Bank 1994: 21–23). About 50 percent of the region's foreign trade is intraregional today. This figure is higher than in any other region except for Western Europe. Japan has a very strong position with a share of both exports and imports of more than 50 percent. However, the largest single bilateral trade flow goes from China to Hong Kong (Lloyd 1994). Today much of the intraregional trade is also intraindustry or even intrafirm trade, often based on foreign direct investment and suggesting a comprehensive business network across national borders.

## CHANGING SPECIALIZATION

In Chapter 2 it was suggested—with the aid of the "Flying Geese" model— how the structure of a country's foreign trade is likely to change with economic development. (In itself, of course, the notion that economic development and structural change are intertwined processes is far from new.) Less developed countries typically export agricultural products and other raw materials (and import manufactures), while more developed countries tend to have a much higher share of manufactured exports. Among the latter, the most developed countries tend to have a concentration of exports in capital goods, that is, machinery and transport equipment, which are technology and skill intensive.

By following the behavior of trade specialiZation on primary goods, "other" manufactures and "machinery and transport equipment" (these categories were defined to cover all exports), we are able to obtain a rough picture of the level of development of different East Asian countries and changes in that level over time, as elaborated at a theoretical level in Chapter 2. According to the "Flying Geese" model, differences in development are conducive to regional development as a whole. Additionally, and what really amounts to much the same thing, we will get an idea of complementarities in the region. The instrument used in the following exposition is the so-called specialization index, constructed as

$$S_{ik} = \frac{X_{ik} - M_{ik}}{X_{ik} + M_{ik}}$$

where $X_{ik}$ is country i's exports of product group k, and $M_{ik}$ is country i's imports of product group k. The value of the index obviously varies between -1 (no specialization) to +1 (complete specialization). Figure 3.1 shows the development of the index for the three product groups mentioned above for a number of East Asian countries. (Countries left out are not included due to data problems.)

As Figure 3.1. shows, most East Asian countries have roughly accommodated the specialization pattern suggested in Chapter 2, based on the "Flying Geese" framework, even though there are discrepancies, sometimes substantial ones, due to particular conditions in the economies concerned. In the case of Japan, specialization displays a structure typical for an advanced stage of development. The transformation to the industrialized country stage took place about 1970, using the criterion focusing on trade specialisation proposed in Chapter 2. In Korea, this stage is just being reached, while Taiwan by now also fulfills the condition for an industrialized country. The city-states, Hong Kong and Singapore, may be somewhat difficult to compare to other countries. In the former case, the status of industrialized economy seems to be on the verge of fulfillment. Hong Kong has lately become more and more a service economy, however, where industrial production is losing in importance. After 1997, this trend, if anything, will probably be strengthened. Singapore largely fulfills the criteria for a developed economy.

For both Hong Kong and Singapore, specialization in primary goods behaves differently from what is predicted by the "Flying Geese" model. This is not surprising, however, as the *production* of primary goods is almost nil in both countries. Singapore's status as a base for FDI strongly affects its production and trade structure. Hence the status of industrialized country was achieved in the early 1970s, although trade specialization on "other" manufactures is still on the increase, too. Indonesia is still clearly in the developing country category, although the "young NIC" stage should be reached fairly soon.

**Figure 3.1**
**Export Specialization in East Asia**

**Japan**

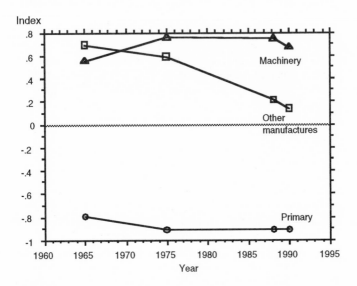

**Korea**

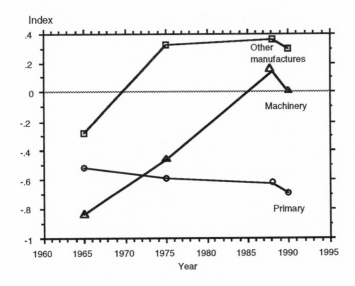

Figure 3.1 continued

**Taiwan**

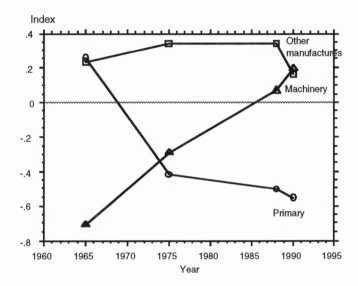

**Hong  Kong**

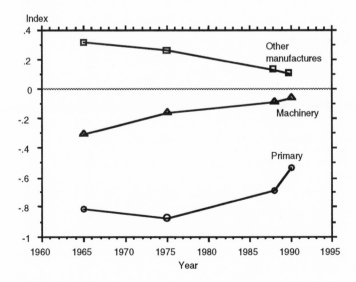

Figure 3.1 continued

## Singapore

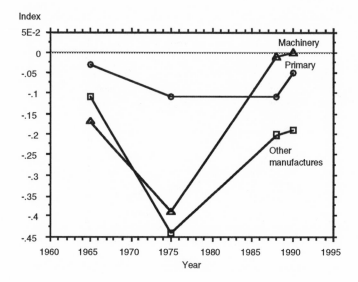

## Indonesia

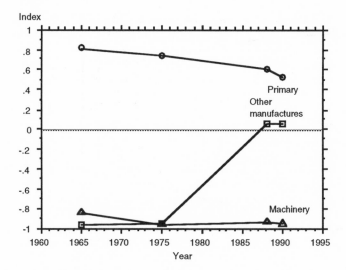

Figure 3.1 continued

**Philippines**

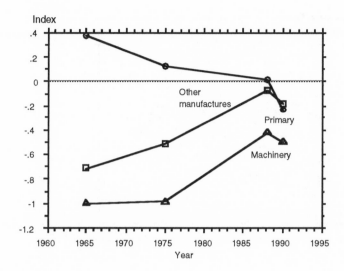

**Thailand**

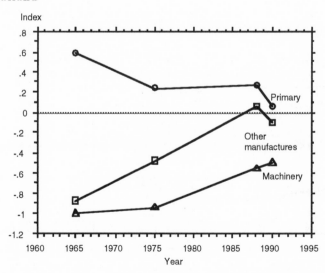

Figure 3.1 continued

**Malaysia**

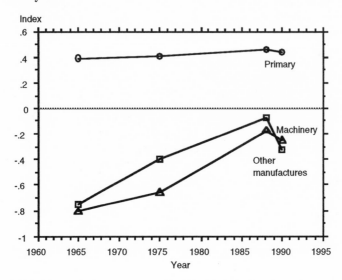

**China**

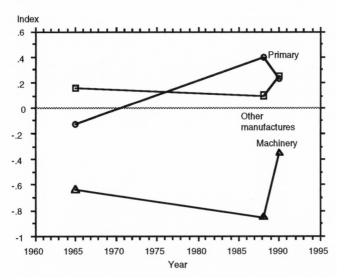

*Note:* Primary goods are SITC categories 0–4 and 68; Machinery comprises SITC category 7.
Other manufactures comprise sections 5–9 minus section 7 and division 68.
*Source:* adapted from Kwan 1994: 88.

Malaysia is very much a special case due to its continuing strong specialization on primary goods, even during the last thirty years of strong industrialization. The reason for this is, of course, the country's exceptionally rich endowment of natural resources. Apart from this, the country's industrial structure is quite advanced, with a higher index value for machinery than for "other" manufactures. The Philippines, in turn, has just arrived at the "young NIC" stage, while Thailand, despite a much higher GDP per capita, seems to lag somewhat behind. In the case of Thailand, a similar picture as for Malaysia is conveyed, in the sense that ample resource endowments keep primary goods exports high, even if the country is industrializing rapidly. China, finally, went though fundamental changes after the late 1970s, when the economic reforms commenced, a process that is still going on. Hence one should be extremely cautious in drawing conclusions from its trade figures. The main impression of the figure, that China seems to have reached a "young NIC" stage, seems adequate, though.

In order to gain a deeper understanding of the determinants of intraregional trade, we need to examine the trade flows at a more disaggregated level. Particularly, it is of interest to form an idea of what type of goods are exported to or imported from what countries, since in such a way we may draw some conclusions about to what extent the principle of comparative advantage has been realized in the region.

Since, according to the "Flying Geese" model, export and import structures should be different depending on the trade partner's level of development, and since mid-level, "newly industrialized" countries have perhaps the most interesting position in that model, playing the role of both less developed country (LDC) and advanced country simultaneously, the export and import structure of the Asian NIEs (except Taiwan, as comparable data were not readily available) are scrutinized next. This is done in a slightly enlarged framework, the so-called ESCAP (Economic and Social Commission for Asia and the Pacific) region. (That region encompasses, apart from East Asia, also the non-Asian Pacific countries and South and Central Asia. Most of the countries included in the three latter groups are rather insignificant, however, as far as international trade is concerned.)

According to our model, a NIE should be expected to export technologically simple manufactures to both developed and developing countries and, in addition, more advanced manufactures (mostly capital goods) to LDCs. In return, it can be expected to import capital goods from its developed trade partners and raw materials and so on from LDCs. While this can be assumed to be the dominant pattern, reality is never that clear-cut. Hence we have to expect some advanced goods to be exported to developed countries, and some raw materials to be exported to both developed and developing countries. One of the reasons for interpretation difficulties is, of course, statistical. Especially when a crude classification is used, it is more than likely that the same product group contains both simple and more sophisticated products. Despite this, a decomposition of regional exports and imports does convey some information, accounted for in Table 3.2.

With minor exceptions, the results are fairly expected, against the backdrop of the "Flying Geese." As for trade with developed countries, the high share of imports of machinery is striking. On the export side, the share of "other" manufactures is very large, as expected, for Hong Kong and Korea but much smaller for Singapore whose export structure is more advanced, partly due to the exceptionally large FDI, with more than 40 percent of its exports to developed countries in machinery. Singapore is also atypical in the sense that its export share of primary goods is also very large, despite the fact that the republic's resource endowments are close to nil. The large share is explained mainly by the fact that oil refining is a very important export industry in Singapore. Moreover, the country's traditional role as an entrepôt contributes to this result. The table

Table 3.2
Structure of Intraregional Trade: Hong Kong, Korea, and Singapore (percentages)

|  | Hong Kong | | Korea | | Singapore | |
|---|---|---|---|---|---|---|
|  | Exports | Imports | Exports | Imports | Exports | Imports |
| **Developed** | | | | | | |
| **ESCAP** | 100.0 | 100.0 | 100.0 | 100.0 | 100.0 | 100.0 |
| **Primary** | 10.3 | 6.3 | 19.4 | 14.7 | 35.1 | 5.7 |
| **Other** | | | | | | |
| **Manufactures** | 71.6 | 36.9 | 59.6 | 36.6 | 21.4 | 27.9 |
| **Machinery** | 17.8 | 54.6 | 20.9 | 47.4 | 41.2 | 64.8 |
| **Developing** | | | | | | |
| **ESCAP** | 100.0 | 100.0 | 100.0 | 100.0 | 100.0 | 100.0 |
| **Primary** | 8.3 | 10.7 | 8.3 | 56.5 | 29.4 | 25.8 |
| **Other** | | | | | | |
| **Manufactures** | 55.4 | 64.4 | 57.1 | 25.6 | 27.2 | 26.7 |
| **Machinery** | 35.1 | 23.8 | 34.0 | 17.7 | 42.0 | 47.2 |

*Note*: Countries included in the ESCAP region are listed in ESCAP (1994). The product categories are: Primary goods: SITC 0–4; Other manufactures SITC 5, 6, and 8; and Machinery SITC 7.
*Source*: Compiled from ESCAP (1994).

also elucidates Hong Kong's character of a center for light industry—today the territory is predominantly a service economy—with a low export share for machinery. From outside the table it may be noted that there used to be a "triangular" trade relationship between Japan, the NIEs, and the United States, in that the NIEs import capital and intermediate goods from, predominantly, Japan and use the United States as the chief market for the output of finished goods (Kwan 1994: 106–109). The last few years have witnessed a breakdown of this pattern due to the increasing availability of capital and intermediate goods from local sources or other Asian countries, and due to the decreasing importance of the American market as an outlet for Asian exports of finished goods because of trade friction and appreciating exchange rates in Asia (cf. Kwan 1994: 109–110), but also because of increasing purchasing power within the region.

For trade with developing countries the picture is rather similar. "Other manufactures" dominate exports from Hong Kong and Korea, even if the figures are smaller than for the exports to developed countries, but machinery is also important in this case. Korea's imports from LDCs is dominated by raw materials, which are more important than for the case of developed countries. The latter observation holds for Hong Kong and Singapore as well. Singapore's trade structure again deviates from the others: on the export side, machinery dominates, but raw materials are important in this case, too. Also on the import side, machinery dominates, however. This may partly reflect foreign direct investment from the region in Singapore, but available figures are too scant to allow any definite conclusion.

Since comparative advantages are not given, once and for all, a country's optimal trade and production structure can be assumed to change over time, as discussed in detail in Chapter 2. Structural change is sometimes a painful process, since we cannot assume that factors of production can be freely transferred from contracting industries to expanding ones. Hence one may expect some unemployment in the process. FDI, while increasing the capital stock of a country, normally leads to a deficit on the current account at its early stages, and may well cause trade friction, as has been the case to some extent between Japan and the NIEs, especially at times when the latter have not been able to compensate deficits in their trade with Japan with surpluses with third countries (cf. Kwan 1994: 39–40).

The benefits of efficient resource allocation can be assumed to be spread out among the population, and improvements are not necessarily perceived by the single individual, though the gains for the society at large may be great. The losers, however, are likely to be a well-defined rather small group, and the loss per individual may be considerable. This group will therefore probably try to lobby for protection and may also succeed due to the lack of an effective countervailing power (cf. Blomqvist 1989: 71). This may explain some of the reluctance that can be observed when one studies the history of deregulation of trade in the Asia-Pacific region. Since inflexibility of goods and factor markets on the one hand, and the activities of lobbies on the other hand, are two of the most important reasons for pursuing trade policy in the first place, we now turn to a brief survey of trade and industrialization policies.

## TRADE POLICIES

Trade policies, especially in developing countries, are traditionally analyzed within the framework of import-substituting versus export-promoting policies. As well known, the standard "explanation" for the successful development of the East Asian countries is their allegedly outward-oriented policy stance which several of them adopted long before the academic community had fully realized the inherent problems with import substitution. Other countries have embarked on the export-oriented strategy much later, however, and in several of them the rate of protection is still considerable. (For some general expositions on trade and development strategies, see, e.g., Greenaway and Milner 1993 and Krueger 1993.) Taken as a whole, the East Asian developing countries are a good deal more open than most other LDCs.

## Import Substitution versus Export Orientation

During much of the postwar period, the predominating development and industrialisation strategy all over the world was import substitution, that is, domestic industrial production should be substituted for imported products. Hence a country's dependence on exports of raw materials in exchange for processed products would decrease, according to the argument. In order to provide sufficient incentives to potential domestic producers, trade barriers were an essential part of the package, as was also a hands-on approach by the government, often including extensive central planning.

The main factual backup of this basic philosophy was, on the one hand, the experience of many developing countries during the Great Depression in the 1930s and during World War II. Low levels of demand caused the terms-of-trade to fall drastically during the Depression, making it more and more costly to acquire necessary imported consumption and capital goods. During the war again, international trade routes were often cut off or severely disturbed by warfare activity. Peacetime products were scarce as well due to the fact that all major Western economies were tied up in the war effort and their economies geared toward production of military equipment.

The empirical experiences were subsequently supported and generalized by early development economists. According to them, a falling long-term trend could be expected for the prices of commodities, eventually aggravating the terms-of-trade problem in the LDCs. It was therefore paramount for these countries to sever, or at least reduce, their dependence on developed countries by building up a domestic industrial potential. Trade barriers against competition from developed countries were recommended, but also cooperation and market integration with other LDCs. It was generally realized that trade barriers would cause a welfare loss in the short run. The idea was, however, that once the "infant" industries had grown up and become internationally competitive, the protective barriers could be removed. The attitude to FDI was ambiguous to begin with, as it was realized that such investment could help build up industrial capacity. Subsequently, as it became clear that foreign firms often tended to be more efficient and thus outcompete their domestic rivals, the attitude became decidedly negative. Possible political influence through the MNCs was resented as well.

As experience from import substitution accumulated, it gradually became obvious that this policy did not fulfill what was expected of it. Even theoretically, it is not difficult to demonstrate weak points in the argument for tariff-protected industrialization (see, e.g., Södersten and Reed 1994: 258–60). In practice, the worst problem was that the policy, once in place, turned out to be very difficult to dismantle. Moreover, distortions caused by the original interventions tended to cause new problems that also had to be addressed. Eventually the economies became more and more entangled in a web of regulations with very negative effects on growth and development.

Import substitution is basically founded on the notion that markets are imperfect, and thus government intervention is required to rectify the situation. This implies that central planning and control have to be applied along with import substitution. Licensing of imports and foreign exchange were common in countries relying on this strategy, as was central allocation of, for example, raw materials and capital. Interventions in the markets for factors of production were the order of the day as well. Typically, the cost of capital was artificially reduced, in order to encourage investment, which led to excessive capital intensity in production and often to unemployment as well. Relatively high wages in the urban areas attracted labor from the countryside, contributing to uncontrolled growth of the cities and a growing informal sector.

The high level of ambition (often combined with rent-seeking by the ruling elite) tended to inflate government expenditures, which more often than not led to high rates of inflation. Inflation, in turn, caused balance of payments problems which were often addressed with more regulations instead of adjusting the exchange rate. In fact, the exchange rate was often overvalued deliberately in order to keep the prices of imported necessities down. At the same time, of course, exports were discouraged.

Bureaucratic red tape slowed down decision making, and in order to cope with a large number of decisions, the public administration—even if it were honest— frequently had to apply simple decision rules. This tends to preserve the prevailing industrial structure and to hamper innovation and establishment of new enterprises. Small and midsized firms, in particular, tend to be discriminated against. The production possibility frontier of the economy never expands, which was the leading idea of the import substitution policy in the first place. The most profitable activity for firms becomes lobbying for more protection and other favors. This is a "directly unproductive profit-seeking activity" (Bhagwati 1978), reducing the capacity for productive activities even further.

Typically, consumption goods have been the first type of imports to be replaced by domestically produced products, while imports of inputs and capital goods have been continued on favorable terms. Import substitution was supposed to be extended later to the latter type of goods as well, through "linkage effects." This proved to be difficult, however, since domestic inputs are usually both more expensive and qualitatively inferior to imported goods, at least to begin with. Hence there would be a conflict between producers of consumption goods and producers of intermediate and capital goods. The outcome is often a situation where the *effective* protection is higher for final goods than for production inputs.

Import substitution has often, paradoxically, increased dependence on the rest of the world. While the strategy does reduce the demand for foreign exchange directly, the imports of capital and intermediate goods lead to an increase. Since import substitution discourages exports, the end result may well be negative. Furthermore, remaining imports tend to become more and more critical for the functioning of the economy. Imports of consumption goods can be fairly easily cut down in a crisis, but prohibition of imports of, say, spare parts and vital inputs would bring the economy to a virtual standstill (cf. Blomqvist and Lundahl forthcoming).

Today it is quite clear that the import substitution experiment, by and large, was a disaster. For the countries that embarked on that strategy, backing out is difficult, however, partly because they are left with an industrial structure incompatible with the country's comparative advantages, and partly because the strategy has left a heritage of strong and politically influential pressure groups which resist unfavorable changes in their privileged situation. Hence it is not surprising that the emerging alternative to import substitution, export-led development, at first took root in some small and midsized Asian countries where the traditional power structures had been destroyed by war or other serious international conflicts or where the future of the states as independent entities was otherwise severely threatened due to a hostile political environment. In that situation, a strong economy became a precondition for the survival, not only of the incumbent rulers, but of the state itself.

The basic philosophy of the export-led strategy is that exports to the world market are to be the driving force of an economy's economic growth (see, for instance, Hong 1990). In the first Asian NIEs, this was a logical strategy to employ, since these countries were very resource-poor and had limited domestic markets. Hence neither exports of commodities nor import-substituting industrialization were viable alternatives for sustained development. Still, in the early 1960s, exposition to the vagaries of the world market was not what most leading academics and development agencies recommended. Perhaps the greatest achievement of Lee Kuan Yew, Park Chung Hee, and Chiang Kai-shek was that they realized what was a workable strategy long before the academic profession had arrived at the same result. (The details of the strategies in different countries were rather different, though, even if the basic idea was similar.)

The concept itself, "export-led" development strategy, has been given different interpretations. The most common one is, simply, that the concept denotes an undistorted free trade solution (cf. Bhagwati 1978). Sometimes the concept has been given a stronger meaning, however, a distortion *in favor* of exports. Even in the former case, some government intervention may be necessary, considering that exports usually are more risky and take place within a more uncertain environment than domestic sales. Such measures often cause direct costs to the states, for instance, in the form of subsidies. Hence the government is likely to discontinue its support as soon as possible.

In reality, export incentives have frequently been given through the factor markets, for example, as subsidized interest rates or tariff exemptions on imported intermediate goods. In that case, distortions of factor markets have been introduced, with welfare losses—at least in the short run— as a consequence. For example, in Korea, subsidised interest rates have been combined with comprehensive regulations of the capital market in favor of the export industry. The result was not always very good as consequences frequently included overinvestment, financial difficulties, and restructuring (Blomqvist and Lundahl, forthcoming).

A third strategy, more and more popular over time, has been to lure foreign firms to invest in the country, with the aid of various incentives, such as tax holidays, provision of infrastructure, and assistance with training of the labor force. Singapore, of course, is the paramount example of this strategy. In this country, the largest share of the industrial output is still produced by foreign firms, although considerable spillover effects have taken place. In order to take full advantage of FDI, the foreign trade regime, as well as the domestic markets should be reasonably undistorted, however, as suggested, for example, by the "Flying Geese" model in Chapter 2. (Convincing empirical evidence for this was recently presented by Balasubramanyam, Salisu, and Sapsford 1996.) Fulfilling this condition is likely to increase the volume of FDI (since the products would be internationally competitive) and make them more efficient (since they would operate in an undistorted environment). A competitive environment will ensure that the investments are at the right "level," as far as the present technological competence of the host country is concerned. This is likely to encourage various linkage effects as well (Blomqvist and Lundahl, forthcoming).

The incentives offered to direct investors do not usually distort product nor factor prices. Instead, they tend to affect establishment costs favorably, via tax rebates and access to infrastructure and trained labor. The effect is also diminishing establishment risk, from the point of view of the investor.

Despite the observations above, it is certainly possible to be overzealous in export promotion as well. The problem for the government is not only to perceive the dynamics of comparative advantage correctly in order to know where the encouraging measures should be introduced. Even if this is done correctly— which is easier if a country is still lagging behind the technological front line— international business cycles may cause short-term disturbances and failures even when the policy pursued is "correct" in a long-term perspective. The Korean effort to promote heavy and chemical industries in the late 1970s and Singapore's initiative to increase the wage level in the mid-1980s are cases in point (cf., for instance, Rhee 1994: Ch. 3; Balassa 1991: 79). Both were probably based on a correct perception of an optimal structure of the economy. Timing turned out to be wrong in both cases, however.

## LIBERALIZATION OF TRADE

The developments in the intraregional trade and capital flows, to a great extent, have been a consequence of substantial liberalization of trade, both in the East Asian region and worldwide. The export drive in East Asia has frequently been combined with protectionist policies in the home market.[1] Thirty years ago, the only free traders of any significance were Hong Kong and Singapore. Malaysia and Taiwan opened up somewhat later and to a lesser extent, while Japan's position has been notoriously difficult to assess due to the untransparency of the Japanese system where nontariff measures allegedly play a great role. Hence sharply differing views on Japan's trade policy stance have been expressed over the years. Korea started relatively late, too, but has opened up to a significant extent since the early 1980s. The socialist countries in the region were, of course, extremely inward-looking, while the large ASEAN countries have been liberalizing their policies over time, but often very cautiously and backtracking from time to time.

For the majority of the countries in the region, serious liberalization began only in the 1980s and much remains to be done (cf. World Bank 1994: Ch. 3). Most of these countries are important commodity exporters but, using earnings from their commodity exports, also developed a domestic import-substituting industry, more or less protected from international competition. Indonesia chose to rely on government-linked firms and regulated investment heavily. The collapse in the oil price in the 1980s forced the country to change its policy, however, toward a more open trade regime and a much more positive attitude toward FDI (Okamoto 1995). Today export-led growth is a buzzword in the whole region. Compared to the situation just a decade ago, the commitment in principle to liberalizing trade is now  sincere and virtually unanimous. This does not mean, however, that countries have not reversed their policy from time to time, often as a result of pressure from domestic industry. Especially the nominally socialist countries in the region, China and Vietnam, still exert heavy controls on trade.

**Present Trade Barriers**

The prospects for increasing trade are significantly affected by prevailing trade barriers. In ASEAN, the smaller members—Brunei, Singapore and Malaysia—have liberal trade regimes, with few exceptions. The larger member countries—Indonesia, the Philippines and Thailand—have higher trade barriers, even if these countries have also liberalized their trade to a very significant extent during the 1980s and 1990s, and the trend is expected to continue.

In Indonesia, the *effective* rate of protection[2] in manufacturing was, on average, 52 percent in 1992, down from 68 percent as late as 1987. Especially foodstuffs and the machinery sector have high rates of effective protection, 120 and 82 percent, respectively (World Bank 1994: 36). In the Philippines, quantitative restrictions have been prevalent in a large number of cases. In 1980, 3,000 items (making up 36 percent of customs categories) were affected. This figure decreased to 150 (equal to 2.5 percent of customs categories) in 1992. Agricultural goods and automotive products were the most important in the restricted category.  Thailand's pattern of protection was somewhat similar. About 100 product groups were affected by quantitative controls, including some textiles, some machinery, motor vehicles, paper, and chemical products. Thailand has worked toward replacing quantitative measures with tariffs, and the overall protectionist stance has become considerably milder. The newest member of ASEAN, Vietnam, still has considerable trade restrictions—even though, for example, machinery and equipment are not subject to significant tariffs (World Bank 1994: 35–38).

Table 3.3 summarizes the degree of protection in ASEAN. (From the point of view of an exporter, it must be kept in mind, however, that averages may not be very informative, as trade barriers for single products may be very variable. The situation may also change very quickly. The general trend is thus more

Table   3.3
Trade  Barriers  in  ASEAN

| Country | Unweighted average nominal tariff, percent | Import items subject to import restrictions | Effective protection rate in manufacturing |
|---|---|---|---|
| Brunei (1992) | 5 | .. | .. |
| Indonesia (1992) | 18 | <5 | 52 |
| Malaysia (1992) | 12 | <5 | 28[a] |
| Philippines (1992) | 18 | <5 | 32 |
| Singapore (1992) | 0.36 | 0 | .. |
| Thailand (1992) | 23 | <5 | 51[b] |

.. = not available.

[a] for 1988

[b] for 1988; agroprocessing excluded; weighted by value added in world prices.

*Source:*  Compiled from World Bank 1994: 33; ASEAN 1995: 16; GATT 1992: 79.


important to notice than specific figures.)

In the rest of the region, the situation differs considerably. In Japan, most concern seems to be about informal trade barriers, which may replace dismantled formal barriers. Japan still has considerable tariff barriers, too, in certain areas, such as agriculture, but also in industries such as textiles, footwear, and paper. Korea has an unweighted tariff rate of about 10 percent for all products, while the effective rate of protection in manufacturing was 28 percent in 1988. Also in this case, agricultural products are rather heavily protected, and nontariff barriers are not unusual (World Bank 1994: 33–36).

In Taiwan, the average nominal tariff is about 9 percent, but is substantially higher for some goods, notably agricultural products. Also some industrial goods are rather protected, such as automotive products. Import licensing is still used for a few products as well.

China has gone through a period of very rapid and substantial reform, also in the realm of foreign trade. Despite the reforms, however, the trading system in the country is still centralized with official approval required for all exports and imports (Srinivasan 1994). Although trade barriers have been reduced, significant import restrictions still remain. Strong administrative controls which were imposed on imports in mid-1985 have not disappeared. Such controls have led to the imposition of arbitrary and discretionary import restrictions (Elek 1992). The average nominal tariff rate is not high, however. According to the World Bank

(1994: 35), it is only 5.6 percent of the value of imports, mostly due to various rebates and exemptions. Import tariffs range, however, from 3 percent on promoted imports to over 200 percent on discouraged imports such as automobiles (USIS 1994). The *effective* rates of protection may often be high, since the exemptions are usually applied to raw materials and inputs.

Other studies suggest that China still uses an intricate system of tariff and nontariff administrative controls to implement its industrial and trade policies. Although tariffs on selected products have been reduced, China still uses prohibitively high tariffs in combination with import restrictions and foreign exchange controls to protect its domestic industry and restrict imports. Many products are subject to quantitative restrictions, to import licensing requirements, and also taxes and value-added taxes (USIS 1994).

In 1992, tariffs on 225 items were reduced from an average of 45 percent to 30 percent and the import regulatory tax was abolished. China pledged, effective January 1, 1994, to reduce tariffs on 2,818 items by an overall average of 8.8 percent. It also agreed to eliminate 75 percent of import licensing requirements over a two-year period. At the recent Asia-Pacific Economic Cooperation (APEC) summit in Osaka, the country pledged to reduce its trade barriers again, to a substantial extent. While tariffs have been reduced, and apparently will be reduced more in the future, China continues to use standards and certification requirements as barriers to trade, although it committed itself to eliminate this practice in some areas (Blomqvist and Roy 1996).

## THE GEOGRAPHICAL PATTERNS OF TRADE

Next, we are going to look into the pattern of intraregional trade. After the recession in the early and mid-1980s, major restructuring of the East Asian economies has been taking place. Liberalization has, of course, been one important reason for this. However, exchange rate realignments have been instrumental for changing specialization and trade patterns in the Asia-Pacific region during the last decade or so (Kwan 1994: 13–14). Especially the so-called Plaza Accord in September 1985 was significant, as it led to massive FDI and consequent changes in trade flows. The changing exchange rates may not change the basic effect of changing comparative advantage, though (Blomqvist 1990), but may have speeded up changes that would otherwise have been more gradual .

In Table 3.4, three alternative measures of intraregional trade are given, covering the last quarter of a century. These measures are: intraregional trade as a percentage of global trade, intraregional trade as a percentage of the region's total trade, and the so-called trade intensity index, which, in effect, measures the share of intraregional trade adjusted for the world market share of the region. (Hence, if the intraregional trade remains the same when the region's share of world trade increases, trade intensity goes down.)

Table 3.4 reveals several interesting facts. First, the weight of intra-East Asian trade, related to either global trade or regional trade, has increased strongly during the period under study. In particular, the former measure indicates a strong relative expansion. Extensive trade liberalization, especially in the 1980s, no doubt is one of the paramount reasons for this development, particularly since the largest countries in the region, such as China, Indonesia, and Thailand, were heavily involved in this process. (Many of the smaller countries in the region already had fairly open trade regimes at that time.) Considerable scope for

**Table  3.4**
**Intraregional  Trade  in  East  Asia**

|  | 1969 | 1979 | 1985 | 1990 |
|---|---|---|---|---|
| Intraregional Trade as Percentage of Total World Trade | 2.9 | 4.2 | 6.4 | 7.9 |
| Intraregional Trade as Percentage of Regional Trade | 29.3 | 33.2 | 36.3 | 40.7 |
| Trade Intensity Index* | 3.0 | 2.6 | 2.1 | 2.1 |

* Computed as $I_{ij} = (T_{ii}/T_i)/(T_i/T_w)$, where $T_{ii}$ = intraregional trade, $T_i$ = region's total trade and $T_w$ = world trade.
*Source:* Adapted from World Bank 1994: 25.

liberalization remains, however, especially where nontariff barriers are concerned (World Bank 1994: 32–40).

Somewhat puzzlingly, however, trade *intensity* rather seems to display a negative trend, even if this trend seems to have leveled off in the 1980s. This means that intraregional trade barely has kept pace with the region's share of global trade.  According to this result, the reason for increasing intraregional trade has been the growing weight of the region in world trade. There has not been any increasing bias toward the region's own products, perhaps opposite to the common belief.  Still, it must be added that the trade intensity index for East Asia is larger than for any other comparable region, Western Europe included (World Bank 1994: 25). From this it can be concluded that the degree of trade interdependence in fact is very high in the region, although the trade intensity has not recently been rising as a consequence of the region's global weight. As a matter of fact, as argued by the World Bank (1994: 26), the share of intraregional trade in a region's total trade is probably the most relevant of the measures employed above, at least from a policy point of view.

Tables 3.5 and 3.6 present the structure of total commodity trade between the Asian-Pacific countries, and between those countries and some important extraregional trade partners in more detail.

On the export side, Table 3.5 tells us that East Asia has a very strong position as an export market for all included countries and groups of countries, with an export share between 40 and over 50 percent throughout (slightly lower for Japan, though). Over time this share has been stable or rising. The United States in most cases receives about 20 percent of total exports, except for Japan where the share is larger, about one-third. The share of Europe (that is, the European Union) has been rather small, 10–15 percent in most cases, with an

Table 3.5
Export Matrix for East Asia (percentages)

| Destination→ Exporter | Japan | Korea | Hong Kong | Taiwan | China | Vietnam | ASEAN 6 | East Asia | USA | EC | World |
|---|---|---|---|---|---|---|---|---|---|---|---|
| **Japan** | | | | | | | | | | | |
| 1980 | n.a. | 4.1 | 3.7 | .. | 3.9 | 0.1 | 10.1 | 21.9 | 24.5 | 14.0 | 100.0 |
| 1987 | n.a. | 5.8 | 3.9 | 4.9 | 3.6 | 0.1 | 6.8 | 25.1 | 36.8 | 16.6 | 100.0 |
| 1993 | n.a. | 5.3 | 6.3 | 6.1 | 4.8 | 0.2 | 13.7 | 36.4 | 29.5 | 15.7 | 100.0 |
| **Korea** | | | | | | | | | | | |
| 1980 | 17.4 | n.a. | 4.7 | .. | .. | 0.1 | 6.5 | 28.6 | 26.4 | 15.5 | 100.0 |
| 1987 | 17.8 | n.a. | 4.7 | 1.2 | .. | 0.0 | 4.2 | 27.8 | 38.9 | 14.0 | 100.0 |
| 1993 | 13.8 | n.a. | 7.7 | 2.7 | 6.2 | 0.9 | 11.2 | 42.5 | 21.7 | 10.7 | 100.0 |
| **Hong Kong** | | | | | | | | | | | |
| 1980 | 4.6 | 1.2 | n.a. | .. | 6.3 | 0.2 | 11.2 | 23.4 | 26.1 | 22.9 | 100.0 |
| 1987 | 5.1 | 2.6 | n.a. | 3.2 | 23.3 | 0.1 | 6.2 | 40.5 | 27.9 | 15.8 | 100.0 |
| 1993 | 5.2 | 1.7 | n.a. | 2.7 | 32.4 | 0.4 | 5.8 | 48.1 | 23.1 | 15.0 | 100.0 |
| **Taiwan** | | | | | | | | | | | |
| 1980 | .. | .. | .. | n.a. | .. | .. | .. | .. | .. | .. | .. |
| 1987 | .. | .. | .. | n.a. | .. | .. | .. | .. | .. | .. | .. |
| 1993 | .. | .. | .. | n.a. | .. | .. | .. | .. | .. | .. | .. |
| **China** | | | | | | | | | | | |
| 1980 | 22.2 | .. | 24.0 | .. | n.a. | .. | 6.6 | 52.8 | 5.4 | 13.0 | 100.0 |
| 1987 | 16.2 | .. | 34.9 | .. | n.a. | .. | 5.9 | 57.0 | 7.7 | 9.9 | 100.0 |
| 1993 | 17.2 | 3.1 | 24.1 | 1.6 | n.a. | 0.3 | 5.1 | 51.4 | 18.5 | 12.8 | 100.0 |
| **Vietnam** | | | | | | | | | | | |
| 1980 | 28.2 | 2.6 | 12.8 | .. | .. | n.a. | 10.9 | 54.5 | .. | 10.3 | 100.0 |
| 1987 | 3.1 | 0.0 | 24.6 | .. | .. | n.a. | 5.0 | 32.7 | .. | 8.8 | 100.0 |
| 1993 | 5.7 | 2.7 | 4.2 | 4.6 | 3.7 | n.a. | 17.6 | 38.5 | .. | 19.6 | 100.0 |
| **ASEAN 6*** | | | | | | | | | | | |
| 1980 | 29.6 | 1.5 | 3.4 | .. | 1.0 | 0.4 | 18.1 | 54.0 | 16.4 | 12.5 | 100.0 |
| 1987 | 21.0 | 3.1 | 4.2 | 2.5 | 2.2 | 0.0 | 19.1 | 52.1 | 21.2 | 13.6 | 100.0 |
| 1993 | 15.4 | 3.3 | 5.6 | 3.8 | 2.4 | 0.7 | 20.8 | 52.0 | 20.2 | 14.9 | 100.0 |

* This group comprises ASEAN members during 1984–1995: Brunei, Indonesia, Malaysia, the Philippines, Singapore, and Thailand.
*Source*: Compiled from International Monetary Fund, *Direction of Trade Statistics*, various issues.
.. = Data not available.

Table 3.6
Import Matrix for East Asia (percentages)

| Origin→<br>Importer | Japan | Korea | Hong Kong | Taiwan | China | Vietnam | ASEAN 6 | East Asia | USA | EC | World |
|---|---|---|---|---|---|---|---|---|---|---|---|
| **Japan** | | | | | | | | | | | |
| 1980 | n.a. | 2.2 | 0.4 | .. | 3.1 | 0.0 | 17.4 | 23.1 | 17.4 | 5.9 | 100.0 |
| 1987 | n.a. | 5.4 | 1.0 | 4.8 | 5.0 | 0.1 | 13.1 | 29.4 | 21.2 | 11.8 | 100.0 |
| 1993 | n.a. | 4.9 | 0.8 | 4.0 | 8.6 | 0.4 | 14.2 | 33.0 | 23.2 | 12.6 | 100.0 |
| **Korea** | | | | | | | | | | | |
| 1980 | 26.3 | n.a. | 0.4 | .. | 0.1 | .. | 6.6 | 33.5 | 21.9 | 7.3 | 100.0 |
| 1987 | 33.3 | n.a. | 1.0 | 1.9 | .. | .. | 7.0 | 43.5 | 21.4 | 11.2 | 100.0 |
| 1993 | 23.7 | n.a. | 1.1 | 1.7 | 4.7 | 0.1 | 10.0 | 41.3 | 21.3 | 11.8 | 100.0 |
| **Hong Kong** | | | | | | | | | | | |
| 1980 | 23.0 | 3.5 | n.a. | .. | 19.6 | 0.1 | 7.7 | 53.8 | 11.8 | 12.3 | 100.0 |
| 1987 | 19.0 | 4.5 | n.a. | 8.8 | 31.1 | 0.2 | 7.1 | 70.7 | 8.5 | 11.0 | 100.0 |
| 1993 | 16.6 | 4.5 | n.a. | 8.8 | 37.5 | 0.1 | 8.2 | 75.7 | 7.4 | 9.8 | 100.0 |
| **Taiwan** | | | | | | | | | | | |
| 1980 | .. | .. | .. | n.a. | .. | .. | .. | .. | .. | .. | .. |
| 1987 | .. | .. | .. | n.a. | .. | .. | .. | .. | .. | .. | .. |
| 1993 | .. | .. | .. | n.a. | .. | .. | .. | .. | .. | .. | .. |
| **China** | | | | | | | | | | | |
| 1980 | 26.5 | .. | 2.9 | .. | n.a. | .. | 3.4 | 32.8 | 19.6 | 14.4 | 100.0 |
| 1987 | 23.3 | .. | 19.5 | .. | n.a. | .. | 4.8 | 47.6 | 11.2 | 16.8 | 100.0 |
| 1993 | 22.5 | 5.2 | 10.1 | 12.5 | n.a. | 0.1 | 5.8 | 56.2 | 8.6 | 13.9 | 100.0 |
| **Vietnam** | | | | | | | | | | | |
| 1980 | 14.2 | 1.1 | 3.7 | .. | .. | n.a. | 8.5 | 27.5 | 0.1 | 28.4 | 100.0 |
| 1987 | 32.4 | .. | 12.0 | .. | .. | n.a. | 6.2 | 50.6 | 4.2 | 14.1 | 100.0 |
| 1993 | 9.2 | 14.8 | 10.4 | 10.2 | 5.6 | n.a. | 29.5 | 79.8 | 0.1 | 11.2 | 100.0 |
| **ASEAN 6*** | | | | | | | | | | | |
| 1980 | 21.9 | 1.7 | 1.7 | .. | 2.7 | .. | 18.5 | 46.4 | 15.4 | 12.7 | 100.0 |
| 1987 | 22.4 | 2.5 | 2.7 | 4.2 | 3.7 | .. | 18.6 | 54.2 | 15.0 | 14.0 | 100.0 |
| 1993 | 24.6 | 4.0 | 2.7 | 4.7 | 2.5 | 0.3 | 18.3 | 57.0 | 15.2 | 13.4 | 100.0 |

* This group comprises ASEAN members during 1984–1995: Brunei, Indonesia, Malaysia, the Philippines, Singapore, and Thailand.
.. = Data not available.
Source: Compiled from International Monetary Fund, Direction of Trade Statistics, various issues

unclear trend. ASEAN is almost equally important, except for China and Hong Kong which are each other's most important trade partners.

On the import side, Japan is again the country least dependent on East Asia, but for the other countries and groupings, the region stands for between 40 and 80 percent, and the shares have typically been rising over time. The share of the United States varies between almost nil (Vietnam) and 23 percent (Japan)—in almost every case the import share is substantially lower than the export share of the United States. The share also typically displays a falling trend, with the exception of Japan and, possibly, ASEAN. The share of the European Community (EC) has been fairly similar across countries and groupings at between 10 and 15 percent. Trendwise, however, the variation has been great. In the case of Vietnam, ASEAN's position is remarkably strong, in the virtual absence of the United States, about 30 percent. Intra-ASEAN imports are close to 20 percent of the grouping's total imports but would be much lower if Singapore were not included.

The obvious importance of intraregional trade does lend some superficial support to the popular notion of an emerging Asian-Pacific trade bloc—even if it is formally unorganized—and certainly points to the fact that the region is rapidly becoming more resistant to protectionist tendencies in Europe and the United States. It is also clear that the outward-oriented development of East Asia in general was greatly facilitated in the first place because of the increasing openness of the global trading system (cf. World Bank 1994: 5). This increasing openness has been reflected in the region's trade regimes as well, even if some countries went for liberalization rather recently. The trend in East Asia has clearly been toward liberalizing trade during the last few decades, however, contrary to the trend in most other parts of the world (Bergsten and Noland 1993: 11). Nevertheless, considerable potential for increase in intraregional trade should still exist, since the East Asian countries have continued to apply—to a greater or lesser extent—different trade barriers. Some of the remaining trade barriers are quite untransparent, too, such as government support of various industries and restrictions on competition (Young 1993: 121). According to some measures, it is still at a lower level than in Europe (cf. World Bank 1994: 5), which points to some potential for expanding intraregional trade still further. Besides, trade surpluses earned by several countries in the region have been recycled in the region in the form of FDI, overseas official development aid (ODA), and imports (Cronin 1992: 19).

## Intraindustry Trade

The extent of intraindustry trade may shed more light on the pattern of foreign trade in the East Asian region. Basically, trade between two countries at very different levels of development should be assumed to be mainly of the interindustry kind, the LDC exporting mainly unprocessed goods and importing manufactures including capital goods. (What intraindustry trade there is, can often be explained by the fact that products requiring widely differing factor intensities may be classified as belonging to the same standardized international trade classification (SITC) group. Final products and parts and components used in manufacturing of those products are a case in point.)

The exchange between countries at a similar level of development can be assumed to contain more intraindustry trade. This is because consumer preferences are heterogeneous, but often similar in two countries at the same level of development, while there may well be scale economies in production. Such a combination is likely to lead, as is well known, to national specialization *within* industries. Empirically, this should show up as increasing intraindustry trade when (a) the income level in two countries rises and (b) when the relative income difference between them shrinks. The higher income level, the higher share of manufactures in exports, the smaller income difference, the more similar are consumers' tastes in the two countries (Kwan 1994: 95).

However, pinpointing intraindustry trade empirically is difficult as the picture is blurred by the fact just mentioned, that production of final goods and their components usually belongs to the same SITC class (unless the degree of disaggregation is very high), even if the factor intensities in their production may differ greatly. (Different factor intensities for different product components is, of course, the main reason why many Asian firms have been locating parts of their production process abroad). Thus intraindustry trade may contain trade flows due to complementaries in both production and consumption. In order to be able to say more about the character of intraregional trade in a particular instance, much more detailed research is required.

Langhammer (1989) calculated an index of intraindustry trade between groups of East Asian countries. As a measure he used the Grubel-Lloyd index.[3] Langhammer calculated values for the index for six pairs of countries/pairs of countries for the time period 1965–1985: Japan/NIEs (Korea, Hong Kong, and Taiwan), Japan/ASEAN (including Singapore), Japan/China, NIEs/ASEAN, NIE/China, and ASEAN/China. For Japan/NIEs, Japan/ASEAN, and NIEs/ASEAN, intraindustry trade grew strongly as a percentage of total trade, being 60 percent or more in 1985. In the of cases Japan/China and NIEs/China, the trend has been negative. The reason for this is probably the economic reforms in China, which may have contributed to a restructuring of trade in a direction predicted by comparative advantages. In the case of Japan/China the decrease of the value is especially strong, from 35 to 6 percent. For ASEAN/China, finally, the trend has been positive, but the level in 1985 was still not higher than 39 percent. Note that the measure of intra-industry trade is dependent on the level of aggregation (the higher degree of disaggregation, the less intraindustry trade). The absolute values of figures are thus less interesting than time trends and differences between trade partners.

The general impression is thus a rising trend in intraindustrial trade, in spite of some exceptions. (This trend is of course related to the increasing role of manufactures in the exports of all Asian-Pacific countries; see, e.g., Balassa 1991: 6–11.) The high level of intraindustry specialization in 1985 between ASEAN and Japan and the NIEs, respectively, can probably be explained by the above-mentioned tendency to relocate simpler component fabrication to countries with lower production costs, from where they are exported or reexported to the home country ("take-back" industries). This tendency is now also obvious between the NIEs and ASEAN and China, respectively, but this cannot be

Table  3.7
Intra-industry  Trade  in  Manufacturing  between  the  East  Asian
Countries  and  All  Other  Countries  on  the  List

|  | 1980 | 1985 | 1989 |
|---|---|---|---|
| Japan | 36.9 | 32.1 | 40.9 |
| Korea | 46.5 | 48.5 | 49.3 |
| Hong Kong | 56.7 | 53.2 | 56.2 |
| Taiwan | 38.6 | 43.0 | 54.1 |
| Indonesia | 11.1 | 19.2 | 27.3 |
| Malaysia | 34.4 | 60.1 | 64.0 |
| Philippines | 18.3 | 30.9 | 46.6 |
| Singapore | 63.2 | 73.0 | 72.1 |
| Thailand | 32.1 | 37.5 | 45.1 |
| USA | 65.1 | 60.4 | 64.1 |
| Canada | 64.1 | 69.9 | 63.5 |
| Europe* | 65.3 | 68.0 | 71.4 |

*Note:* The Grubel-Lloyd index is calculated at the two-digit level of SITC.
* "Europe" here stands for France, Germany, Britain, and the Netherlands only.
*Source*: Adapted from Dobson 1993: 32.

assumed to show up yet in figures for 1985. The including of highly industrialized Singapore in the ASEAN group is likely to have an upward effect on the degree of intraindustry trade between ASEAN and Japan and the NIEs, respectively. The general impression of the figures is that they are rather high. To a great extent this can be explained by the fact that the level of aggregation is quite high, too.

Dobson (1993) made similar calculations based on a higher degree of disaggregation, but measuring intraindustry trade between single countries and a group of East Asian countries and other important trade partners. Selected results are reproduced in Table 3.7.

Although the results are not quite consistent, the general trend here also appears to be upward. In general, the proportion of intraindustry trade is higher the higher the development level of a country. Note, however, the comparatively low level of intraindustry trade in the case of Japan, which may well reflect the alleged impenetrability of the Japanese markets. In Asia, Singapore and Malaysia reach levels of intraindustry trade similar to those of Western industrialized countries.

## CONCLUSIONS

This chapter has made a few important observations. First, the weight of East Asia in world trade has been increasing over the long term and is also likely to do so in the future, considering the rapid rates of growth in the region and the trend toward further liberalization of the economies in the region. There is no doubt that foreign trade has been the paramount engine of growth in East Asia— hence most of the countries are good examples of the export-led development strategy by now— although it is too simplistic to maintain that this "explains" the high growth rates. The role of intraregional trade is also very important—in fact increasingly so—even if different ways of measuring this trade convey somewhat different messages and different economies all have characteristics of their own. Particularly, trade-intensity based  measures give a somewhat more sober picture than the others, indicating that the increase in intraregional trade is due more to the fact that the regional economies have grown rapidly than to increasing preferences for products made in the region. It is likely that the latter phenomenon will be more important from the early 1990s on. This is because of the intense intraregional FDI activity which has taken place during the last decade and which has created a network of productive activities. Much of such trade, of course, will be intrafirm trade. Increasing levels of intraindustry trade are likely to be evidence of this process, but are also a consequence of higher income levels and higher technological capability.

Following up the behavior of a specialization index over time for the economies involved here, it is possible to draw some conclusions on the position of each economy as far as its general level of development is concerned. It turns out that several of the East Asian economies are on the verge of reaching or have already reached a position as a developed country, while others lag behind, more or less. This setup should have been (and still is) ideal for a "Flying Geese" type of development to take place. A closer look at the trading patterns of three NIEs seems to support this idea, too.

## NOTES

1. According to Greenaway and Milner (1993: 7), it is not possible to pursue both import substitution and export orientation simultaneously, since export and import competing industries compete for the same factors of production. With less than full resource utilization, a combination of both strategies is conceivable, however.

2. The effective rate of protection gives a measure of protection of domestic value added, i.e., ERP = $(VA_d - VA_w)/VA_w$, where $VA_d$ and $VA_w$ are value added at domestic and world prices, respectively (see, e.g., Greenaway and Milner 1993: 79).

3. The Grubel-Lloyd index is defined as:

$$IIT = \frac{\sum_i (X_i + M_i) - \sum_i |X_i - M_i|}{\sum_i (X_i + M_i)} \cdot 100$$

where $X_i$ and $M_i$ denote exports and imports of product i, respectively.

# 4

Determinants of Bilateral Trade
Flows in East Asia: A Gravity
Approach

## INTRODUCTION

As shown in the preceding chapters, the degree of economic interdependence in the East Asia region has been on the increase during the last few decades in spite of the fact that almost no formal attempts at integration have been made.[1] According to the "Flying Geese" model outlined in Chapter 2 this is because neighboring countries at different levels of economic development tend to develop a trade and foreign investment pattern where the differences in comparative advantages of each country to a great extent drive the trade and investment flows, while changes in such advantages will be reflected in a changing pattern of trade and investment flows over time. This pattern may be further exacerbated if foreign aid is used in order to enhance economic exchange within a region. In order for a "Flying Geese" pattern to emerge, the trading system has to be reasonably liberalized. Otherwise the comparative advantages of different countries would not necessarily materialize in the interaction between countries with consequent trade and investment flows.

Using fairly formalized methods, this chapter investigates the determinants of the bilateral aggregate trade flows in East Asia. Specifically, a modified version of the well-known "gravity model" of foreign trade was employed, originally put forth by Tinbergen (1962) and Pöyhönen (1963), and developed, above all, by Linnemann (see, e.g., Linnemann 1966). Specifically, this model will be combined with elements from the standard neoclassical, Hechscher-Ohlin model of trade.

The model is estimated separately, on a cross-section basis, for three points in time—1971, 1981, and 1989—in order to detect possible trends and to follow up changes in the significance of different variables. The time dimension can also give us some idea about factors "responsible" for the very large increases in the intraregional trade volumes that have taken place during the last few decades.

While this model does not explain economic development as a consequence of (free) trade, but rather the other way around, it is rather obvious that the causal direction here goes both ways: trade fuels development and development fuels trade.

East Asia, in this chapter, is limited to Japan, South Korea, Taiwan, Hong Kong, China and ASEAN (excluding Brunei and Vietnam).[2] The exclusion of Indochina, Burma, and Brunei is due to statistical problems and/or a low level of integration in the regional economy, and should not have any significant consequences for the results.

## THEORETICAL FRAMEWORK

The "gravity model"[3] is aimed at explaining trade volumes (or values). It cannot, in its basic form at least, explain what goods are exported and imported, respectively, which has been the traditional focus of international trade models. The gravity model has most often been used to evaluate the effect of different trade policy measures, such as economic integration, on the trade flows between the countries concerned (see, e.g., Aitken 1973 and Brada and Mendez 1983).

A basic version of the gravity model can be stated as equation (4.1):

$$(4.1) \qquad T_{ij} = f(\underset{+}{Y_i}, \underset{+}{Y_j}, \underset{-}{P_i}, \underset{-}{P_j}, \underset{-}{D_{ij}})$$

(The signs beneath the symbols denote expected signs of the partial derivatives, that is, the direction of effects of changes in the explanatory variables.) Equation (4.1) states the hypothesis that the total trade between country i and country j ($T_{ij}$) is a function of the size of both economies ($Y_i$, $Y_j$, reflecting production and absorption capacity, respectively) and the distance between the economies, a variable which is assumed to capture the combined effects of "transport costs, transport time and economic horizon" (Aitken 1973).

Additionally, except for the two basic variables—economic size and distance between trade partners—the populations of the two countries, $P_i$ and $P_j$, are usually included as explanatory variables as well. The rationale for this is that the population is supposed to function as an approximation of potential scale economies. The idea is that population determines market size, and the larger market size, the more industries have a "sufficient" domestic market in terms of being able to produce at the minimum efficient scale.[4] Thus the expected effect on trade volumes is negative for both the domestic and the trade partner's population.

The basic framework of equation (4.1) may be elaborated—often with the aid of dummy variables—in order to allow, for instance, for country-specific characteristics and policy measures, as will be demonstrated in the empirical part of the chapter.

Although the gravity model has performed very well indeed in empirical studies—at least in terms of fit of the model—its theoretical underpinnings have usually been considered somewhat shaky. Linnemann (1966) has shown, however, that an expression similar to the gravity model can be deduced from a competitive general equilibrium model. A comprehensive treatment of the issue is provided by Leamer and Stern (1970: Ch. 6). (Prices cancel out because they are assumed to be endogenous and adjust quickly to equalize supply and demand; cf. Leamer and Stern 1970: 146–147.) An expression similar to the gravity model can also be derived from a probabilistic transaction model with a variable included that captures trade "resistance," as in work by Savage and Deutsch (1960) (cited in Leamer and Stern 1970: 158).

An obvious weakness of equation (4.1) is that differences in comparative advantages do not enter into the equation in any way. It would be natural to assume that small differences in comparative advantages lead to smaller trade flows than great differences, *ceteris paribus*. The approach taken in this chapter is to take this point of view into account explicitly.

A notorious problem when testing traditional (e.g., Ricardian and neoclassical) trade models is the fact that they are difficult to translate into an empirically testable form (cf. Deardorff 1984). These models also, in their standard form, explain the *direction* of trade, not quantities. There is a way out, however, first envisaged by Leamer (1984). The starting point is Vanek's (1968) extension of the standard theory to the case with many factors of production. Vanek sees foreign trade as an exchange of factor services, embodied in the traded products, a view that renders the exact composition of exports and imports less interesting.[5]

In Vanek's analysis, comparative advantage is constituted by a country's relative abundance of factor endowments relative to the global endowment. Then, if two economies are related to each other, the "world component" cancels out and we obtain a measure of relative abundance between the two economies as:[6]

$$(4.2) \qquad R_{ij}^{k} = \frac{F_{i}^{k}/F_{j}^{k}}{Y_{i}/Y_{j}},$$

where $R_{ij}^{k}$ is the measure of relative abundance of factor k (k = 1, . . ., m). $F_{i}^{k}$ and $F_{j}^{k}$ are the endowments of factor k in country i and j, respectively, and $Y_{i}$ and $Y_{j}$ are production capacity in the two countries. If $R_{ij}^{k} > 1$, factor k is more abundant in country i; if $R_{ij}^{k} < 1$ the factor is more abundant in country j. Now the assumption is that the trade flow is larger the greater the relative factor abundance is. When total trade is the variable to be explained, the absolute deviation from unity ($|R_{ij}^{k} - 1|$) is what counts; the larger the differential, the more trade regardless of which way the differential goes. Using (4.2), the model for explaining total trade between i to j would be:

$$(4.3) \qquad T_{ij} = g(\underset{+}{|R_{ij}^{1} - 1|}, \ldots, \underset{+}{|R_{ij}^{m} - 1|})$$

(The expected signs of the partial derivatives are given beneath the variables.)

The formulation in (4.3) has some obvious shortcomings, however, just as the gravity model. First, the size of the economies involved does not enter the model, and must thus be considered an implicit *ceteris paribus* condition. Second, a model like (4.3) cannot be supposed to explain intraindustry trade, that is the portion of gross exports that is replaced by imports of similar goods.[7] Leamer (1984) estimated a model similar to (4.3) using *net* exports as a percentage of GDP and thus managed to avoid these two problems. The method used here is to merge the traditional trade model with a "complete" gravity model instead of only using GDP as a scaling variable.

Combining equations (4.1) and (4.3) gives the complete "hybrid" model in a theoretical form:

$$(4.4) \qquad T_{ij} = T_{ij}[f(Y_i, Y_j, P_i, P_j, D_{ij}), g(|R_{ij}^1 - 1|, \ldots, |R_{ij}^m - 1|)]$$

## THE EMPIRICAL STUDY

For the empirical work we used a log-linear version of (4.4), amended with a few dummy and quasi-dummy variables identified below:

$$(4.5) \qquad \ln T = b_0 + b_1 \ln LAND + b_2 \ln TROP + b_3 OIL + b_4 \ln HUC + b_5 \ln LF + b_6 \ln IR + b_7 \ln D + b_8 \ln Y + b_9 \ln P + b_{10} TP + b_{11} HK + b_{12} SPORE + b_{13} ADJ + b_{14} ASEAN + u.$$

The dependent variable, $\ln T$, stands for total trade exchange between countries $i$ and $j$. The explanatory variables (leaving out subscripts and using the symbols for the different factors of production as denoting relative endowments for notational simplicity) are: LAND, relative endowment of land; TROP, relative availability of tropical land; OIL, relative endowment of oil resources; HUC, relative endowment of human capital; LF, relative endowment of labor; IR, relative capital abundance; D, the distance between $i$ and $j$; Y, the combined domestic national product of a pair of countries; P, combined population of a pair of countries; TP, "openness" of trade policy, combined for each pair of countries; HK, a dummy for trade flows between Hong Kong and China; SPORE, a dummy for trade flows between Singapore and other members of ASEAN; ADJ, a dummy for adjacent economies; and ASEAN, a dummy for intra-ASEAN trade; u, a residual. (For an exact description of proxies used, see the Appendix.)

The role of most explanatory variables above is fairly self-explanatory. However, a few of them require some elaboration. TP, which takes values from 1 ("very open") to 4 ("very protected"), is intended to take into account the trade policy stance of trading countries. HK is a dummy variable, designed to capture the fact that much of China's foreign trade, including trade with countries with which China does not (or did not) uphold formal relations, is recorded as trade with Hong Kong. Singapore has a somewhat similar role as an entrepôt in Southeast Asia, which the dummy SPORE is assumed to pick up. ADJ is included to take account of various effects of common borders, such as "local" trade, registered as foreign trade, similar tastes, superior information on market conditions, and so on (cf. Aitken 1973). ASEAN, finally, is included in order to capture possible trade effects of ASEAN's cooperation programs (cf., e.g., Blomqvist 1993 and Chapter 7 in this volume).

The model was estimated in a logarithmic form[8] (except for the dummy variables, and for TP, which is also a quasi-dummy), a solution that was not based on any particular theoretical considerations but which gives a superior fit. As usual in this context, the data is cross-section, although collected for three different years, 1971, 1981, and 1989.

Some of the theoretical concepts we need for this analysis are difficult to capture in a readily measurable form. If only for this reason, we have to keep in mind that the results are tentative. The weakest of the proxies used are probably the measure of human capital, HUC, and the physical capital abundance, IR. In the former case, we used the proportion of the relevant age group enrolled in tertiary education. Except for the fact that this is an obviously incomplete measure of the theoretical concept—as other forms of education and training should matter as well—the comparability of the figures across countries may be less than perfect. IR stands for a ten-year average of the ratio of gross investment to GDP (the ten preceding years to the one for which the estimations are made are used). While this is hardly an ideal measure, the available alternatives, such as adding gross investments over the preceding years and deducing estimated depreciation, are not necessarily much better and much more laborious.

The distance between two countries is of course not a well-defined concept. For one thing, the actual transport routes are seldom equal to a straight line between two points. Second, the end-points of such a line are by no means always self-evident. In general, the distance between the capitals should provide an acceptable measure, since the capital is usually also the economic center of a country. For the case Hong Kong and China, there is an obvious problem, though. We chose to measure the distances to Guangzhou instead of Beijing, Guangdong Province now being the economic powerhouse of China. The distance to other countries were measured from Guangzhou as well.[9]

The proxy for trade policy is very rough, treating in effect an ordinal scale as an interval scale. The technique saves degrees of freedom, however, compared to the alternative of using pure dummy variables. We have not tried to correct the official values for the GDP according to purchasing power parity, but we did transform all dollar values into 1989 prices in order to make a comparison of the coefficients over time meaningful.

In the data, observations of trade between China and Taiwan and Korea, respectively, are missing due to the fact that there was no official trade in the years under scrutiny. (Some de facto trade is likely to be included in trade involving third countries, which, to some extent, may distort the data. The dummy for trade between Hong Kong and China was introduced partly for this reason, to minimize possible effects of this.) In 1971 there was no reported trade between China and the Philippines and Thailand, respectively, either, so these observations had to be omitted. Singapore does not report its trade with Indonesia separately, so we have to use data reported by Indonesia only. The free-on-board (f.o.b.) Singapore export value is estimated to be 90 percent of the Indonesian import value, following Imada et al. (1992: 5). Using total bilateral trade and allowing for the missing observations just identified, we have 43 observations altogether (41 for 1971).

## RESULTS

Before running the regression model (using the ordinary least squares method [OLS]), we checked for possible collinearity between the explanatory variables. Since the correlation between lnLAND and lnLF was rather high (although spurious), and a preliminary regression run failed to produce significant coefficients for either of them, we left out the former variable in order to avoid a multicollinearity problem.[10] Some preliminary runs also showed that the other resource variables, lnTROPIC and lnOIL, were consistently insignificant, so they were left out of the final estimations. Differences in natural resource endowments hence do not seem to be important as an explanation of the intraregional trade in East Asia.[11]

The results of the runs of the model (equation (4.5) minus lnLAND, lnTROPIC, and lnOIL) are reported in Table 4.1. As usual with gravity models, the "explanatory" value of our model was very high, the adjusted $R^2$ ranging from 0.88 in 1971 to 0.85 in 1981 and 0.91 in 1989.

Of the comparative advantage variables, only those related to human resources, lnHUC and lnLF, seem to be important for Asian-Pacific intraregional trade. According to this result, differences in educational levels and the endowment of "raw" labor are the principal comparative advantage-based determinants of trade. Capital abundance was also significant in 1971 but totally insignificant for the two other years. The variance of this independent variable (IR) is rather small, which may make the establishing of a relation between such a variable and the dependent variable difficult. Another possible explanation is perhaps more interesting: the mobility of capital in the region has increased significantly during the last few years, a fact that is likely to lead to a more even distribution in relative capital abundance.[12] If that is so, the endowment of capital does no longer constitute a basis for comparative advantage. The other factors of production are much less mobile, if at all. (Intraregional capital mobility was insignificant in 1971, which may be the explanation for the significance of the variable for that year.)

The gravity variables came through very strongly in the analysis. (As a matter of fact, when we left out the comparative advantage variables altogether in a tentative regression run for 1989, the coefficient of determination fell only slightly.) They all had the expected sign and were all highly significant. Surprisingly enough, the dummy variables failed to take significant coefficients (with the possible exception of SPORE in 1981). Hence, controlling for other determinants of trade, the roles of Hong Kong and Singapore in their respective regions may have been overstated. Interestingly, but not entirely unexpectedly,ASEAN has not had any significant effect on the trade flows between the member countries.

The trade policy variable, TP, seems to be quite important for the trade exchange, and is consistently significant. While this is of course not unexpected

**Table   4.1**
**Regression   Results**

**1971**

| Variable | Coefficient | t-value | P-value |
|----------|-------------|---------|---------|
| Constant | 4.741 | 1.743 | 0.092 |
| lnHUC | 0.317 | 1.936 | 0.063 |
| lnLF | -0.084 | -0.652 | 0.519 |
| lnIR | 1.062 | 1.680 | 0.104 |
| lnD | -0.750 | -2.395 | 0.023 |
| lnY | 0.779 | 6.174 | <0.0001 |
| lnP | -0.164 | -0.649 | 0.5216 |
| TP | -0.740 | -3.215 | 0.003 |
| HK | -0.127 | -0.095 | 0.925 |
| SPORE | 0.773 | 1.204 | 0.238 |
| ADJ | -0.791 | -1.061 | 0.298 |
| ASEAN | -0.074 | -0.135 | 0.893 |

**1981**

| Variable | Coefficient | t-value | P-value |
|----------|-------------|---------|---------|
| Constant | 0.558 | 0.297 | 0.768 |
| lnHUC | 0.641 | 4.260 | 0.000 |
| lnLF | 0.369 | 2.622 | 0.013 |
| lnIR | -0.084 | -0.125 | 0.901 |
| lnD | -0.568 | -2.923 | 0.006 |
| lnY | 1.174 | 8.766 | <0.0001 |
| lnP | -0.916 | -4.886 | <0.0001 |
| TP | -0.299 | -1.980 | 0.057 |
| HK | -0.123 | -0.144 | 0.886 |
| SPORE | 1.107 | 1.943 | 0.061 |
| ADJ | -0.117 | -0.265 | 0.793 |
| ASEAN | -0.263 | -0.705 | 0.486 |

**1989**

| Variable | Coefficient | t-value | P-value |
|----------|-------------|---------|---------|
| Constant | 7.487 | 4.792 | <0.0001 |
| lnHUC | 0.398 | 3.038 | 0.005 |
| lnLF | 0.236 | 3.001 | 0.005 |
| lnIR | 0.172 | 0.322 | 0.750 |
| lnD | -0.794 | -4.652 | <0.0001 |
| lnY | 0.720 | 9.202 | <0.0001 |
| lnP | -0.296 | -2.597 | 0.014 |
| TP | -0.653 | -5.965 | <0.0001 |
| HK | 0.377 | 0.578 | 0.567 |
| SPORE | 0.401 | 0.894 | 0.378 |
| ADJ | 0.186 | 0.511 | 0.613 |
| ASEAN | -0.035 | -0.128 | 0.899 |

in itself, it may suggest that the rather rough proxy we had to use after all is able to capture the essence of the theoretical concept aimed at. Finally, it is remarkable that there are no clear outliers in the observations.[13] This means that the same model, for recent years, is able to capture the trade of China, the only planned economy in the group, and countries like Singapore and Hong Kong with exceptionally unregulated and extensive foreign trade.[14]

As far as the development over time is concerned, it is difficult to discern any trends in the regression coefficients, indicating, for instance, decreasing friction in intraregional trade relations. Presumably, the trade policy variable, in all its oversimplification, manages to take care of this aspect.

It might be of some interest to follow up which of the explanatory variables are "responsible" for the increase in trade volumes that can be observed. According to our data, real intraregional trade flows in East Asia increased about sevenfold between 1971 and 1989. The reason for this increase is not increasing differences in relative factor endowments, since these differences, in fact, decreased during the period for all factors included (HUC, LF, and IR). Since an increasing population is related to decreasing trade, the larger trade flows can only be attributed to the growth of production capacity (proxied by GDP) and to a continuing liberalization of trade policies. (The "black box," the constant term, also increased between 1971 and 1989 but since it was smaller in 1981 than in both those cases, it is hard to give a sensible interpretation to this.)

Since production capacity is hardly independent of trade volumes in the longer run, the two may have strengthened each other. One factor, not explicit in the present model but discussed elsewhere in this book, that may be an important determinant of trade flows, is intraregional foreign investment, which has increased strongly, especially during the 1980s (cf. United Nations 1991: 67–74; 1992). While foreign investment obviously influences our results via both IR and GDP, and indirectly probably via HUC as well, it would not be easy to include that variable explicitly in a model like this, especially since direct investment may create as well as suppress trade, depending on the circumstances (cf. Kojima 1973, 1975, 1985).

Technically, there seems to be no problems with the regressions. The material does not show indications of a serious multicollinearity problem after eliminating LAND. Moreover, the residuals were checked for possible heteroscedasticity, but turned out to fulfill the theoretical requirements for "BLUE" (Best Linear Unbiased Estimator): $E(u) = 0$, $E(u^2) = s^2$.

## CONCLUSIONS

By and large, and keeping in mind the weaknesses inherent in the approach and in the data base, our gravity *cum* comparative advantage model seems to work very well, indicating, for one thing, that the size of the economies concerned and the distance between them are important determinants of trade in the East Asia region. So is the trade policy stance of the countries involved. Furthermore, differences in human capital and labor endowment add significantly to the explanation of the gravity variables. However, ASEAN's role as an integrating factor in the region seems rather insignificant on the basis of this evidence, although of course all aspects of that role cannot be expected to be reflected directly in bilateral trade flows. Hong Kong's and Singapore's roles as regional entrepôts were not corroborated by these results.

The increasing trade flows during the period investigated do not seem to originate in increasing differences in comparative advantages. Rather it seems like the explanation can be found in the continuous liberalization of foreign trade policies in the region, and in the rapid economic growth in the countries concerned. The latter is, however, likely to be a function of expanding foreign trade, at least to some extent and over time. A very tentative interpretation is that we probably have an example of a virtuous circle here: trade liberalization has led to growing GDPs, which have increased savings and investments in industries with a comparative advantage, leading to more trade and growth, and so on. The parallel to Chapter 3 is obvious, where we saw that the different measures of intraregional trade seem to suggest that the observed increase is a result more of the increasing size of the economies concerned than of more intense trade. Foreign direct investment may have been part of the story, too, but its impact cannot be directly deduced from the model used in this study.

In the near future the trend of increasing intraregional trade is likely to continue, except for the fact that the economies of the region are growing as rapidly as ever, because of the obvious unutlized trade potential that can be unleashed by further liberalizing the trade regime. As it seems for now, such continuous liberalization is likely to take place. In that process, East Asia's share of world trade will increase as well.

## APPENDIX: DESCRIPTION AND SOURCES OF VARIABLES

The proxies for relative factor abundance are constructed as in equation (4.2), using GDP for standardizing for size of the economies, with the exception of HUC, which relates university enrollments to the relevant share of the population.

$T_{ij}$: total trade between i and j, f.o.b., US$ millions, (International Monetary Fund, *Direction of Trade Statistics*; Government of the Republic of China, *Statistical Yearbook of the Republic of China*)

$LAND_i$: total area of country i, 1,000 square kilometers (World Bank,*World Development Report*)

$TROP_i$: area with tropical rainy climate, 1,000 square kilometers (Leamer 1984; *The Times Atlas of the World*)

$OIL_i$: oil and natural gas production, 1,000 metric tons (United Nations, *Energy Statistics Yearbook*, 1992; Government of the Republic of China, *Statistical Yearbook of the Republic of China*, 1990). Figures for Taiwan estimated using the conversion factor 0.85 tons/1,000 liters.

$HUC_i$: human resource development, percentage of relevant age group enrolled in tertiary education, closest possible year (World Bank,*World Development Report*, various issues)

$LF_i$: labor force, measured as population in the age group 15–64 (World Bank,*World Development Report*, various issues)

$IR_i$: "capital endowment" (average Investment/GDP for last ten years) (United Nations, *National Accounts Statistics*, various issues)

$D_{ij}$: distance between i and j, kilometers (*The Times Atlas of the World*)

$Y_i$: gross domestic product of i, US$ millions (World Bank,*World Development Report*, various issues and *World Tables*, various issues; Government of the Republic of China, *Statistical Yearbook of the Republic of China*, various issues)

$P_i$: population of i, millions (World Bank,*World Development Report*, various issues and *World Tables*, various issues).

$TP_{ij}$: trade policy, measured as the sum of a quasi-dummy for degree of openness (1= very open, . . ., 4 = very protected) for a pair of countries (World Bank,*World Development Report*, 1987). Figures for 1989 constructed using various available information on trade policy development.

SPORE: dummy for trade flows between Singapore and other ASEAN countries

HK: dummy for trade flows between Hong Kong and China

ADJ: dummy for adjacent economies

ASEAN: dummy for trade flows between two ASEAN countries

## NOTES

1. The only exception is the Preferential Trade Agreement within the Association of Southeast Asian Nations (ASEAN), a scheme that has had small practical consequences (Blomqvist 1993). This does not necessarily mean, however, that ASEAN's cooperation programs would not be conducive to increasing trade volumes between the member countries. In 1992 ASEAN signed an agreement to create a free trade area, AFTA, within the next fifteen years. (This time frame was later reduced to ten years; see Chapter 7.)

2. That is, Indonesia, Malaysia, the Philippines, Singapore, and Thailand.

3. The term is somewhat misleading in that it is based on a superficial analogy to the gravity phenomenon in physics: two planets are more attracted to each other the larger the mass of the planets is and the closer they are to each other. In economics, there is, of course no automatic parallel (cf. Leamer and Stern 1970:158).

4. Other suggestions inasmuch as population is concerned have also been put forth: Leamer and Stern (1970: 152–153), for example, note that countries with large populations will have their demand structure skewed toward nontradables (due to the need of feeding, clothing, and sheltering the population). On the supply side, countries with small populations will have their production possibilities skewed toward exportables, tend to specialize, and have large volumes of foreign trade. Countries with large populations have, according to Leamer and Stern, production possibilities skewed toward domestic goods and hence have reduced foreign trade sectors.

5. This approach circumvents the notoriously difficult question of relating the factor intensities of exports and imports to the relative factor abundance in the economy under study.

6. I owe the idea for this specific way of modeling comparative advantage to DeRosa (1993).

7. Seeming intraindustry trade may of course often be a manmade phenomenon, created by methods of classification. In such a case, products belonging to the same product class may well be quite different in terms of factor intensity, and the theory of comparative advantages may apply.

8. The logarithm version of the relative factor abundance variables is derived directly from (4.2) as:

$$|\ln R_{ij}^{k}| = |(\ln F_{i}^{k} - \ln F_{j}^{k}) - (\ln Y_{i} - \ln Y_{j})|.$$

9. Arguably, there are other alternatives as well, such as Shanghai.

10. Since LAND is in no way adjusted for the quality of land, this is likely to be the weaker proxy of the two. The other case of a somewhat high correlation is that between lnHUC and lnP. As this does not seem to lead to problems with identifying the two coefficients, we chose to retain both these variables.

11. The likely reason for this result is indeed the fact that we study only the intraregional trade. In a global context the resource-related variables are almost certain to play a role.

12. Qualitative differences in the capital stock in different countries may and do certainly still remain. It is reasonable to assume that capital is partly complementary to other factors of production, so the level of education in particular should be decisive for what form foreign real capital takes.

13. It has to be remembered, however, that several observations including China had to be omitted due to nonexistent (or nonreported) trade.

14. The biggest residuals are for the trade between Taiwan and Korea (trade overestimated) and Hong Kong and Singapore (trade underestimated), respectively.

# 5

## Intraregional Foreign Investment and Development Aid in East Asia

### BACKGROUND

Chapter 2 focused at a theoretical level on, among other things, the interplay between trade flows, foreign direct investment (FDI), and aid in the process of economic development. Looking into the issue of investment somewhat more in detail, we may note that the role of FDI in the development process and industrial restructuring is at least fourfold, apart from that of physical capital injection. First, embodied new know-how in imported capital goods plays a role for the upgrading of domestic production. The multinational companies function as a training ground for prospective domestic managers, many of whom gradually move on to domestic firms, bringing their know-how and management skills with them. For this transfer channel to work, a certain level of management and productive skill, as well as technical flexibility, in the host country are required (cf. Kojima 1977: 152). Thus a host economy may have difficulties in digesting technologies brought in by technically very advanced companies.

Second, industries that grow uncompetitive in a more advanced country may survive by moving their production to less developed neighbors. The tendency to allocate production internationally according to the competitive advantages of different countries is well known (cf., e.g. Porter 1990: 18, 57–58). Such relocation may be facilitated by aid-financed investments in the host country, especially in infrastructure.

An important reason for making an FDI, instead of just selling off the machinery in uncompetitive industries to less developed countries, is knowledge of international markets, access to distribution channels, and other so-called ownership advantages (see Casson 1987: 32–36) that are complementary to the production technology and can be used by the investor in the new location (cf. Riedel 1988). A variant of this pattern is to locate the production of different parts of a vertically integrated industry according to the comparative advantage of each country (Blomström 1990: 7). For this pattern to work properly, the host country has to be reasonably outward oriented in order to allow flexible international exchange of products. Less technology and know-how intensive lines of production in the home country may, for the host country, be activities at the sophisticated end of its product range. Blomström's (1990: 42) results suggest a certain tendency in that direction in the sense that the exports of multinational companies seem to have a bias toward relatively advanced goods. FDI in this case augments the industrial base of the host country, whereas in an inward-looking country the investment may only crowd out domestic firms in the same industry.

FDI is traditionally used as a means of circumventing trade barriers. In that case, too, the point concerning technology transfer is of course relevant. However, in this case there seem to be negative effects in the form of the establishment of monopolies (because the domestic firms often cannot take on the foreign competition, especially as the domestic market is usually relatively small, even in large countries) and the destruction of domestic entrepreneurship (Andersson and Burenstam Linder 1991).

Third, FDI is likely to have secondary effects on the trade flows between investor and host countries, and between the latter and the rest of the world. This is because of the restructuring of productive capacity that FDI contributes to, but also because investment tends to lower transaction costs in international trade by reducing commercial risks, improving marketing know-how, and enhancing information about commercial prospects (cf. Langhammer 1991b). In particular, foreign firms may be a crucial element when firms in a developing country work to establish themselves in the markets of other countries (Blomström 1990: 7). Even if a firm is "competitive," in the sense of being able to produce goods of certain qualities at certain prices, it is often difficult for it to establish itself in the export markets. Increasing international relocation of production will show up in the trade figures as increasing intraindustry and intrafirm trade.

Finally, the intensified competition caused by the entry of a multinational firm may enhance the competitiveness of domestic firms as well, contributing indirectly to larger foreign trade volumes (cf. Blomström 1989: 69–72, 92; 1990: 57). The foreign firm, in its turn, may benefit from being located close to the market, especially in cases where it is important to adapt the product to local tastes, and so on.

## WORLD TRADE REGIME AND FDI

Some important changes in the global competitive environment faced by transnational corporations can be distinguished as having stimulated the emergence of integrated worldwide or regional networks of producing subsidiaries, and defined the potential role of developing country facilities. The most important change is no doubt the lowering of tariff levels through successive rounds of GATT negotiations. This process has radically changed the business environment for both domestic firms in LDCs and for multinational companies. Many host-market subsidiaries have been dependent on tariffs to permit them to remain competitive in those markets. The small size of the markets in LDCs did not permit the foreign affiliates to realize economies of scale fully, in order to reach a level of cost competitiveness that would allow them to compete with imports. Once tariff protection is removed, such affiliates may not be competitive even on the local market. To avoid the economic and political costs of closing down, the firm may seek a more suitable role for such a plant. Integration into a globally coordinated production program implemented by the MNC is one plausible option.

It does not seem likely that the forms of trade restraint incorporated in the so-called new protectionism—which is based on nontariff barriers— are likely to reduce substantially either the need for, or the feasibility of, this form of global restructuring by established transnational corporations. East Asian MNCs (mostly from Japan and the NIEs) are certainly being induced by the new protectionism to establish production facilities in developed countries, but seek as much as possible to supply components to these from specialized subsidiaries in developing countries in order to retain as much as possible of an important element of their established competitiveness. Generally, changes in the nature and distribution of protectionist measures seem to contribute to the growth of globally integrated production networks (United Nations 1992a).

While in general the attractiveness of LDCs as hosts for FDI has deteriorated, the share of Asia in this investment has already been on the increase for some time. The absolute figures have also grown rapidly in the latter case. Hence what happens in the East Asian region is of considerable relevance, also from a global perspective. Surpluses on the current account create a conducive climate for FDIs—important for several East Asian countries—but do not automatically bring them about. There must also be "ownership advantage," that is, the investing firm must have a specific advantage that makes it competitive against host country firms. Cultural familiarity may also play a role, for instance, for the overseas Chinese investment network in Southeast Asia (Hill 1990).

Foreign direct investment is today a major force of market integration in the world economy, as well as in more limited, regional contexts. Until the 1980s, FDI to the East Asian region[1] emanated mostly from the former colonial powers, especially the United States and the United Kingdom. This picture has now changed completely. Today intraregional investment comprises a large share of FDI in the region. A complicated network of firms is emerging, where complementary units are often located in different countries in order to take advantage of differing comparative advantages.

## AIMS OF THE CHAPTER

This chapter provides a picture of how FDI has contributed to the interdependence of the East Asian countries. This is a rather difficult task, empirically, although the problem is not a lack of literature. What would be needed, however, is comparable data per host country and industry for each source country separately, preferably in both stock and flow form. Such data is not readily available.[2] The notorious problem with FDI figures is also the lack of firm international standards for how the investments should be measured.

Consequently, the data actually available are compiled according to differing principles across countries.[3]

Despite these difficulties, it is possible to obtain a rough idea of the ownership networks rapidly building up in the region. The figures given are best interpreted as orders of magnitude, however, due to the problems just mentioned. An additional shortcoming is the fact that the picture keeps changing and the figures available are inevitably several years old even in the best of cases. Hence the current situation may sometimes differ significantly from the one depicted in the data. Even though we may have a rough idea of what changes have taken place, no figures can be given. The chapter is best understood as an attempt to capture and interpret the main developments in the 1980s.

The approach taken in this chapter is "who invests where?" viewing FDI mainly in a context of changing production and trade patterns due to dynamically changing comparative advantages. While it does not attempt to give a formalized theory-based explanation of the realized investments in the region, it does discuss possible reasons for the outcomes, with the "Flying Geese" framework as a theoretical backbone.[4] We will start by giving an overview of the developments in the East Asian region as far as FDI is concerned. We will then scrutinize the investments of Japan, the newly industrialized economies,[5] ASEAN, and China separately. After that, we will look into the industrial distribution of different countries' intraregional FDI. The chapter concludes with a short survey of another type of resource flows, development aid.

## GENERAL TRENDS

The largest FDI flows are between developed countries. Traditionally, that is, up till the 1980s, developing Asia was a relatively small recipient of FDI, even in a less developed country context, but from about 1986 on, the region has grown enormously in importance and had received more than 50 percent of all FDI inflows to LDCs by the end of the decade.[6] FDI in Asia as a whole increased from US$ 3 billion in 1980 to 16.5 billion in 1989. In fact, 95 percent of that amount went to the region discussed in this book: (about 50 percent to the four NIEs, 26 percent to ASEAN, and 19 percent to China (*Transnationals*, December 1991). China is the host country that accounts for most of the increase (UNIDO 1990: 12).

The NIEs, with the possible exception of Hong Kong, have recently been receiving an increasing share of their inward FDI from developed countries. This is most likely due to the availability of skilled labor and the high-quality infrastructure in these countries, combined with reasonable production costs, as compared to the source countries. For developing countries, on the other hand, with their less advanced demands on the skills of the labor force, the NIEs are becoming expensive as sites for affiliates, even if the stable economic and political environment in these countries remains a definite advantage. A reflection of the same reasoning is found in the inward investment in the ASEAN countries (excluding Singapore), where the share of LDC investors is larger, and has increased or remained stable. (Asian investors make up between two-thirds and all of this investment.) In China, LDC investors by now represent the bulk of the country's inward FDI.[7] Malaysia is a similar case, with a very high proportion of its inward FDI coming from countries classified as

**Table  5.1**
**Distribution  of  Inward  FDI  Stock  by  Type  of  Home  Country (percentages)**

| Host country | Year | Developed countries | Japan as % of FDI from developed countries | LDCs[*] | Asia-Pacific[**] as % of FDI from LDC |
|---|---|---|---|---|---|
| Japan | 1990 | 86.7 | n.a. | 13.3 | .. |
|  | 1980 | 94.3 | n.a. | 5.7 | .. |
|  | 1977 | 95.3 | n.a. | 4.6 | .. |
| Hong Kong | 1989 | 83.1 | 36.0 | 16.9 | 88.2 |
|  | 1984 | 92.0 | 22.9 | 8.0 | 76.5 |
|  | 1975 | 84.0 | 18.3 | 16.0 | 39.7 |
| Korea | 1988 | 92.8 | 56.1 | 5.8 | 66.5 |
|  | 1980 | 89.9 | 67.3 | 8.2 | 26.1 |
|  | 1976 | 88.6 | 69.4 | 9.7 | 18.9 |
| Singapore | 1989 | 94.6 | 32.5 | 5.4 | .. |
|  | 1980 | 88.5 | 18.9 | 11.5 | .. |
|  | 1975 | 64.9 | 14.5 | 35.1 | .. |
| Taiwan | 1988 | 72.3 | 37.1 | 27.7 | 61.9 |
|  | 1980 | 63.2 | 29.4 | 36.8 | 71.6 |
| Indonesia | 1988 | 72.8 | 38.2 | 27.9 | 82.8 |
|  | 1980 | 77.1 | 48.6 | 22.9 | 70.6 |
|  | 1975 | 77.7 | 54.6 | 22.3 | 75.4 |
| Malaysia | 1987 | 59.2 | 33.9 | 40.4 | 93.0 |
|  | 1981 | 58.6 | 30.0 | 41.4 | 92.2 |
| Philippines | 1987 | 90.6 | 14.7 | 9.4 | 78.4 |
|  | 1980 | 92.0 | 18.3 | 8.0 | 64.6 |
|  | 1975 | 97.2 | 24.2 | 2.8 | 81.7 |
| Thailand | 1988 | 77.3 | 47.5 | 22.8 | 98.4 |
|  | 1980 | 80.2 | 36.2 | 20.3 | 99.9 |
|  | 1975 | 82.9 | 32.8 | 17.3 | 97.2 |
| China | 1987 | 35.0 | 20.5 | 65.0 | 98.3 |
|  | 1984 | 41.8 | 13.9 | 58.2 | 96.6 |
|  | 1982 | 58.5 | 8.4 | 41.5 | 93.6 |

*Note*: ..= not available, n.a.= not applicable
[*] LDC as defined in note 6.
[**] Defined as East, South, and Southeast Asia and the Pacific island countries (Australia and New Zealand not included).
*Source*: Compiled from United Nations 1992b: 19; United Nations 1993: 30.

LDCs (especially Singapore but also Taiwan and others) (United Nations 1992b: 19). Table 5.1 summarizes this information.

The significance of inward FDI for the Japanese economy is very small, although Japan is one of the leading international actors in *outward* FDI. Also Korea is a small recipient of FDI, while the figures for Taiwan and the smaller NIEs, Hong Kong, and, in particular, Singapore, show much greater reliance on foreign equity capital. The importance of FDI is also comparatively great in Indonesia and Malaysia, but much less so in the Philippines and Thailand.

Also in absolute terms Japan is relatively small as a host for FDI. According to the latest available figure, when this chapter was written, for 1990, the stock of inward investment in Japan was about US$ 16 billion. The information on source countries is scarce, but as Table 5.1 reveals, 87 percent came from other developed countries. Several other countries in the region, with much smaller economies, have attracted more investment than Japan, as is evident from Table 5.2. The high figures for China and some ASEAN countries, especially Indonesia, are perhaps the most interesting facts to be found in this table.

**Table  5.2**
**Inward  FDI  in  East  Asia  (stock  data,  US$  billions  in  1989  prices)**

|             | FDI | Year |
|-------------|-----|------|
| Japan       | 10  | 1988 |
| Korea       | 4   | 1988 |
| Taiwan      | 11  | 1988 |
| Hong Kong   | 3   | 1989 |
| Singapore   | 11  | 1989 |
| China       | 16  | 1988 |
| Indonesia   | 34  | 1990 |
| Malaysia    | 8   | 1988 |
| Philippines | 2   | 1989 |
| Thailand    | 6   | 1989 |

*Sources*: United Nations 1992b; IMF 1992; Government of Singapore, *Singapore's Investment Abroad*, 1976–1989 (1991).

Much of the Japanese and also the NIE investment has taken place in industries where comparative advantage in the home countries has turned less favorable over time (that is, typically in the more labor-intensive industries). In such a case it is often an advantage to locate the foreign investment not too far from the parent company. Especially the possibility of a profitable location of parts of a production process to another country, for "take-back," is not independent of transport costs and costs related to time lags caused by a long distance between two complementary production units (cf. United Nations 1992a: 30). There are reasons for FDI, however, that are unrelated to comparative advantages. Large domestic markets still seem to be of significance, and so is the fact that products from LDCs frequently are granted preferential market access, for example, within the Generalized System of Preferences (GSP).[8]

The pattern of investment is certainly not an outcome of pure economic forces only. Economic nationalism and institutional preconditions play a crucial role, too, even in the source countries. Notwithstanding the general tendency toward liberalization, especially after the recession and falling commodity prices in the mid-1980s, most East Asian countries still have a regulatory framework in place in order to exert control over FDI. This has no doubt contributed to the regional pattern of investment. The former British colonies—Hong Kong, Malaysia and Singapore—have been the most open ones, while Indonesia was almost totally closed to FDI up to the late 1960s, restrictive in the late 1970s and early 1980s, and liberal again after 1985. China's position changed with the economic reforms from the late 1970s, but was of course extremely closed before that. The investment climate in the country today, although positive, relies rather heavily on specific incentives combined with strict control (Chen 1993). The rest of the group takes intermediate positions, with a definite trend toward more liberal regimes (a brief survey of restrictions and future prospects is given in World Bank 1994: Ch. 4).

The mix of incentives and trade barriers on the industry level certainly affects the pattern of inward FDI. For instance, the electronics industry has generally been encouraged to invest for reexport, while the automotive industry usually has aimed at penetrating the host country market behind substantial trade barriers. Finally, for the overseas Chinese, *guanxi* networks may affect the volumes and patterns of investment.

Taiwan, and particularly Korea, were rather reluctant hosts for FDI until the 1980s. Malaysia and Indonesia were already significant hosts before that, but deregulation that took place in the countries in the mid-1980s, concerning demands on local ownership and employment of foreigners, encouraged investment further. In the case of the Philippines, the climate was less than encouraging until the 1970s (Hill 1990). More recently, a major reason for the modest amounts of FDI in this country has been the unstable political situation. The inadequate infrastructure has been, and still is, another impediment. Thailand's FDI regime has been fairly permissive, especially after 1986, with some exceptions. Differing fiscal incentives have been used rather than direct controls to regulate the inflows (Hill 1990; Natarajan and Tan 1992: 8–10).[9]

In addition to the official policy toward FDI, the attitude of domestic capital is of significance. In the past, foreign capital was seldom welcomed by domestic industrialists, who often exerted pressure on their governments to keep foreign investors out, or at least to protect the domestic firms. Moreover, the state capital sector, which is strong in many East Asian countries, generally also used to be less than enthusiastic about potential interference by foreign firms (Phongpaichit 1990: 81–82 and 93–95). For that reason, special economic zones were frequently set up for them, where they could contribute in a limited way to the development of the host country, offering, for instance, employment, but with minimal linkages to the rest of the economy. This reluctant attitude largely changed in the 1980s, as the importance of linkages to the domestic economy became clear, even if there is some pressure for increasing the share of "new" forms of investment, such as technology contracts, at the expense of more traditional forms.

The *sectoral* distribution of inward FDI has undergone significant changes during the last few decades. The primary sector has lost in importance, although it remains a considerable target for investments in resource-rich countries, particularly in Southeast Asia. The share of the secondary sector has increased, first in the NIEs and later in the less developed countries, as the latter have become more attractive as low-wage production sites. The development has been enhanced, as emphasized earlier, by the gradual liberalization of trade regimes. The NIEs remain leading host countries for increasingly advanced production. The share of the tertiary sector in the total stock of FDI has been on the increase, especially in the NIEs, reflecting partly the complementary nature of services and manufacturing and partly a more liberal investment climate for services. In Southeast Asia (minus Singapore), the share of the tertiary sector has not increased, evidently due to the very rapid increase in investments in the secondary sector (United Nations 1992b: 21–24).

The increase of FDI in services in general is easy to understand, keeping in mind the increasing share of services in most national economies and the fact that services by nature are much less tradable than commodities (cf. United Nations 1991: 18–19). Traditionally, FDI in services was severely restricted in most countries, but this was changing rapidly in the 1980s (cf. United Nations 1992b: 8). Increasingly complex manufacturing equipment also makes it necessary to ensure the availability of complementary service facilities. In many cases this must mean that FDI in services has to be made along with investment in industrial capacity. Finally, the development in computer and telecommunications technology, rendering some services more tradeable than before, may lead to a decomposition of the production process in services. Parts of the production of some services can now take place in an LDC. For instance, storage and retrieval of raw data is a labor-intensive process, where the skills required are quite limited. The transmission of such data to or from anywhere in the world is simple and only requires access to the regular telecommunications network.

Despite the increasing role of FDI in East Asia it should be noted that the amounts invested are still mostly small, for example, compared to gross domestic investments, total capital inflows and intraregional trade (cf. Hill 1990; Hill and Johns 1985). For instance, the average annual investment flow to Asia (except Japan) was US$ 3.4 billion during 1981–86[10] (OECD 1989: 50), compared with the total value of intraregional trade, about US$ 110 billion (in 1981). In quantitative terms, FDI makes up only a minor share of total investment in most host countries (Table 5.3). FDI is likely to be much more important than what the quantitative estimates suggest, however, due to its role in diffusion of new technology, including management and marketing know-how (see, e.g., Ruffin 1993). MNCs can also play a crucial role for market access of LDCs, as mentioned earlier.


## JAPAN'S FDI

Japan became an international investor on a small scale in the mid-1950s. The FDI volumes grew through the 1960s, the activity having a strong Asian bias

**Table 5.3**
**FDI Inflows\* as a Share of Gross Domestic Capital Formation (percent)\*\***

|                    | 1980–82 | 1986–87 |
|--------------------|---------|---------|
| Japan              | 0.1     | 0.1     |
| Korea              | 0.5     | 1.4     |
| Taiwan             | 1.0     | 3.3     |
| Hong Kong          | 7.1     | 15.2    |
| Singapore          | 23.4    | 25.5    |
| China              | ..      | ..      |
| Indonesia          | 11.1    | 14.4    |
| Malaysia           | 8.2     | 8.7     |
| Philippines        | 1.6     | 3.5     |
| Thailand           | 2.6     | 2.7     |
| Developed market economies | 2.9 | 3.4 |
| Developing countries | 6.0   | 6.1     |

\* Note that this concept is not exactly identical with FDI (since the latter need not necessarily be synonymous with capital inflows).
\*\* The figures in this table are at variance with those reported in other studies; cf., e.g., Chia 1993. Especially the figure for Indonesia is on the high side, compared to other studies. Unfortunately, it is not clear what the reason is for these discrepancies. No qualitative conclusions in this book are affected, though.
.. = not available.
*Source*: United Nations 1991: 7–8.

(Phongpaichit 1990: 5).[11] (A liberalization of the rules for outward FDI took place in Japan in 1967–1970.) The early investments were concentrated in resources, such as petroleum, lumber, and minerals (Yamazawa 1990: 209). The amounts were not significant until the 1970s, however, when there was considerable investment in textiles and other light industries in other Asian countries (Ichimura 1988: 35; Urata 1991: 176; Yamazawa 1990: 209). As in the late 1980s, the main reason for the increase was an appreciating domestic currency which squeezed profit margins and, at the same time, made foreign assets cheaper than before (cf. Dobson 1993: 10).

Japan's official attitude toward outward FDI was rather negative, with the exception of natural resource extraction. Hence the control of outward capital flows was strict (Dobson 1993: 10). The balance of payment restriction was one reason for this reluctance, at least until the late 1960s (cf., e.g, Urata 1991: 19, 179). However, Japan, being a resource-poor country, had a vital interest in securing a supply of raw materials and energy. In manufacturing, the NIEs were dominating as host countries in Asia especially in the 1960s and 1970s, but their relative share has been declining over time (Phongpaichit 1990: 29).

Later, Japan's role became more global, and also the developed countries have become important as hosts for Japanese FDI, even if Japanese investment still has a clear Asian bias compared to other developed countries (Hill 1990). Japan's share of world outward FDI increased rapidly in the late 1980s, being close to 20 percent for the period 1985–89, for example, up from only 9 percent for the period 1980–84 (United Nations 1991: 10).

The main reason for the increasing activity of the Japanese in the late 1980s was the rapid appreciation of the yen after 1985. The appreciating currency speeded up the process of relocating industrial activities according to comparative advantage. With the increasing purchasing power of the yen, foreign capital goods, land and so on became cheaper, too (cf. OECD 1989: 52). According to a recent study of the World Bank, 6 percent of the production of Japanese manufacturing industries takes place overseas, while the corresponding figures for Germany is 17 percent and for the United States, 23 percent (World Bank 1994: 56). If anything, this indicates that there is still substantial potential for further FDI from Japan in the future.

Another reason for FDI is the threat of limited access for Japanese products in several important markets, which provides an incentive to "change" the country of origin for its products. This has been the reason for much investment in the developed countries, in particular (Urata 1991: 175; Yamazawa 1990: 209–210).

Among the supply side factors propelling Japanese FDI, the increasing restriction in the form of a shortage of land has been mentioned. Finally, and less positive from the point of view of prospective host countries, emerging concerns about the environment have been a reason for some FDI in heavily polluting activities, which thus are removed from Japan (cf., e.g., Phongpaichit 1990: 15, 17).

Table 5.4 reports the cumulative direct investment from Japan for the periods 1951–1982 and 1951–1988, respectively. The real value of Japanese FDI almost tripled between 1982 and 1988. Every single country, or group of countries, according to the classification in Table 5.4, had more Japanese FDI in absolute values in 1988 than in 1982, regardless of shifts in relative shares. Japanese investment going to the East Asian countries as a proportion of Japanese investment to all developing countries increased, even if their share of the country's total investment decreased during the period. Indonesia has traditionally been the most important—no doubt because of the resource richness of that country—a position it has retained even though the increase in investment in the country was rather modest in the 1980s.

The distribution of FDI in different countries says little about the importance of this activity for the host countries. To get a rough idea about this the FDI figure was related to the GDP of the respective country. The result of this exercise is reported in Figure 5.1. Three economies stand out as particularly important hosts in relation to their size: Hong Kong, Singapore, and Indonesia. It is also interesting to notice the rather low levels of investment in Taiwan and Korea in this context. The explanation for this is most likely the rather reluctant attitude to FDI, especially in Korea, until recently (OECD 1989: 51; cf. also Chen 1993).[12] Particularly Japanese FDI has been regarded as less desirable, as a result of historical reasons (Hill 1990).[13] Similar sentiments in ASEAN seem to have receded from the 1980s on. In the case of China there is a great deal of interest on the part of the Japanese, but the FDI volumes are still quite small due to uncertainty about the political stability and sometimes unclear property rights of foreign investors.

**Table 5.4**
Japanese Accumulated FDI Stock, 1951–1982 and 1951–1988 (fiscal years), (US$ billions in 1989 prices).

|  | 1951–82 | | 1951–88 | |
|---|---|---|---|---|
|  | Value | % | Value | % |
| Developed Countries* | 30.074 | 45.7 | 117.321 | 60.6 |
| Developing Countries | 35.808 | 54.3 | 76.376 | 39.4 |
| Korea | 1.627 | 2.5 | 3.378 | 1.7 |
| Taiwan | 0.594 | 0.9 | 1.863 | 1.0 |
| Hong Kong | 2.263 | 3.4 | 6.414 | 3.3 |
| Singapore | 1.715 | 2.6 | 3.964 | 2.0 |
| China | .. | .. | 2.117 | 1.1 |
| Indonesia | 9.012 | 13.7 | 10.196 | 5.3 |
| Malaysia | 0.947 | 1.4 | 1.907 | 1.0 |
| Philippines | 0.894 | 1.4 | 1.165 | 0.6 |
| Thailand | 0.646 | 1.0 | 2.072 | 1.1 |
| Other | 18.110 | 27.5 | 43.299 | 22.3 |
| Total | 65.882 | 100 | 193.697 | 100 |

* Here defined as Australia, North America, and Western Europe.
*Source*: Garnaut 1989: 88; World Bank, *World Tables,* 1992.

Table 5.5 gives an estimate of how the sales of Japanese-owned enterprises in Asian countries were divided between markets in the 1980s. The table shows that the importance of the local market was decreasing during that decade, no doubt because of the continuing trade liberalization in the region. Still, more than 50 percent of the production of the Japanese affiliates went to the local market. Likewise, the proportions going "back" to Japan and to third countries, respectively, were on the increase in the 1980s and were about 16 and 30 percent, respectively, in 1987.

Earlier work (OECD, 1987: 207) suggests, rather expectedly, that the host country market is more important the bigger and more closed that market is. Even in a small open country like Singapore, the Japanese affiliates catered primarily to the domestic market, however. Much of this supply was consumer goods, especially in the 1960s and 1970s, because of trade barriers in most Asian countries (Phongpaichit 1990: 14).

Of the local sales, only 9 percent was intrafirm trade, while 77 percent of the exports to Japan was made up by such transactions. For the exports to third countries, the figure was 24 percent. The scope for intrafirm trade of course differs in different industries, according to the extent the production process can be decomposed into manufacturing of parts. This can usually be done in the machinery industry, while the possibilities in process industries, such as chemicals and metals, are much more limited.

To summarize, the results indicate that the local market is still of great importance when FDI is decided on, but the investments also function as export platforms and as production bases for certain components. The "take-back" of production (measured as share of exports to Japan that is intrafirm trade) is not insignificant but still did not comprise more than about one-eighth of the total, according to the figures for 1987. When measuring intrafirm trade we have to keep in mind the important role of subcontractors in Japanese industrial organization, however. If we would include subcontractors in the entity of a "firm," the share of intrafirm trade would be higher. This is because there has recently been a tendency for small and medium-size enterprises, which largely function as suppliers of intermediate goods to the big companies, to follow the latter abroad where the established cooperation can continue (UNIDO 1990: viii). For a small company this is a low-risk option for establishing itself abroad.

**Figure 5.1**
**Japanese FDI (Stock) in Selected East Asian Countries as Related to Host Country GDP, 1988**

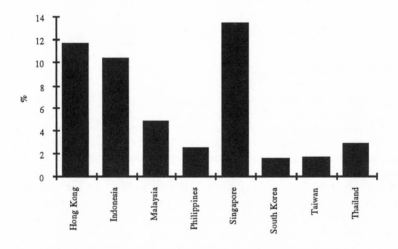

*Sources:* Garnaut 1989: 88; World Bank, *World Development Report 1991;* Government of the Republic of China, *Statistical Yearbook of the Republic of China.*

A fairly high proportion of intrafirm trade also with third countries suggests that the Japanese firms are increasingly resorting to geographical intrafirm division of labour, whereby a specific type of production is located where conditions are most favorable. These emerging networks work as a powerful impetus to regional integration. The pattern is particularly strong in the electrical and electronics industry, and the automobile industry, which together comprise about 50 percent of the sales of the Japanese Asian affiliates (United Nations 1991: 48). As Table 5.6 shows, quite a large proportion of the sales to Japan and third countries by these industries is intrafirm trade. The share is especially high in the exports of electric and electronic equipment to Japan and in

**Table 5.5**
**Sales by Market of Japanese Affiliates in Manufacturing, for Selected Asian Countries, (percentages)**

|      | Host Country Market | Japan | Third Country Market |
|------|---------------------|-------|----------------------|
| 1981 | 63.9                | 9.8   | 26.4                 |
| 1984 | 66.4                | 10.8  | 22.3                 |
| 1987 | 54.7                | 15.8  | 29.9                 |

*Source*: Cronin 1992: 49.

the exports of automobiles (and components) to third countries. As far as purchases are concerned, most inputs are bought in Japan in the electronics and electrical industry, typically as intrafirm transactions. Intrafirm purchases are also common for purchases from third countries, but much less so for local purchases. The same tendency holds for the automobile industry as well. The role of local purchases is naturally highest in resource-intensive industries, but has been on the increase in other industries, too, at least in ASEAN (Phongpaichit 1990: 56).

## FDI BY THE NIES

Except for Japan, FDI from Asian countries was insignificant before the 1980s. The four NIEs have been increasing in importance as foreign investors during the last few years, however. The increasing investment activity has been facilitated by large, in some cases very large, reserves of foreign exchange that these countries accumulated in the 1980s. A contributing reason for the increasing activity was, as in the case of Japan, changing comparative advantages, specifically a shortage of labor which prompted a search for more advantageous production locations (United Nations 1992b: 28). Hong Kong, and especially Singapore, have actively encouraged outward FDI in order to broaden the industrial base of the countries (cf. United Nations 1992b: 27). Also, for the NIEs appreciating exchange rates certainly played a role for pushing out companies with a competitive disadvantage (cf. Baum 1993; Chen 1993; Waitt 1993).

According to available figures, the NIEs accounted for more investment than the Japanese in stock terms in the mid-1980s. Whitmore and Lall (UNIDO 1990: 20) arrived at a figure of US$ 16.9 billion for the four NIEs in East and Southeast Asia alone (in 1985), the corresponding Japanese figure being US$ 12.2 billion. Taiwan had US$ 2.5 billion, Hong Kong US$ 12.2 billion, Singapore US$ 1.8 billion [14] and Korea US$ 412 million (UNIDO 1990: 20–21). When the smaller size of the NIEs is taken into account—the NIEs together have a GDP of less than 20 percent the value of that of Japan—it becomes clear that they invest much more heavily than Japan.

Available FDI figures for the late 1980s suggest that Japan had a stock of investment in the region of about US$ 30 billion (Table 5.4), while the NIEs had some US$ 14 billion (Table 5.7). Thus the importance of the NIEs seems to

**Table 5.6**
**Division of Sales and Purchases of Japanese Asian Affiliates in the Automobile and Electrical and Electronics Industries, 1987 (percentage intrafirm trade in parentheses)**

|  | Automobile Industry | Electrical and Electronics Industry |
|---|---|---|
| **Sales** | | |
| — Local | 74 (9.1) | 43 (9.1) |
| — Sales to Japan | 6 (46.0) | 22 (73.3) |
| — Sales to Third Countries | 20 (62.8) | 35 (32.1) |
| **Purchases** | | |
| — Local | 30 (0.0) | 36 (6.2) |
| — Purchases from Japan | 59 (56.1) | 55 (78.1) |
| — Purchases from Third Countries | 11 (67.9) | 9 (55.9) |

*Source*: United Nations 1991: 49–50.

have declined slightly during the late 1980s, but, considering the uncertainty margin implicit in the figures, no strong conclusions should be drawn. In fact, the figure for the NIEs almost certainly is too low. Recently, particularly the Taiwanese investment has risen sharply, a fact not yet fully taken into account by the figures above. According to Baum (1993), more than 4,000 Taiwanese firms set up subsidiaries in Southeast Asia alone from 1987 on,[15] which amounted to US$ 12 billion or almost half of the total Taiwanese FDI flow in that period.[16] In the early 1990s the country invested heavily in China as well. A similar observation can be made for Korea, too (United Nations 1992b: 29; Waitt 1993).[17] Only in 1990 was Korea's FDI flow about US$ one billion (Waitt 1993). (According to recent figures, the stock of Japanese FDI in the East Asian region was US$ 47 billion in early 1992; Cronin 1992: 11).

The bigger NIEs, Korea and Taiwan, shifted their emphasis to investment in developed countries during the 1980s (Table 5.7). This no doubt happened because of nascent protectionism in the United States and Western Europe. Korea and Taiwan were quite small foreign investors until the late 1980s anyway. From that time, these countries have invested mostly in developed countries (and predominantly in the United States) on the one hand and in Southeast Asia on the other. Hong Kong has increasingly concentrated its FDI in China, in spite of the fact that the colony has many of the same problems with trade barriers in the West as the other NIEs. A similar tendency to invest in nearby sites is evident for Singapore as well, although the heavy concentration on Malaysia was later balanced by investments in other countries, notably in Hong Kong.

The NIEs apparently invest little in the other NIEs, a fact than can be explained by small domestic markets in the host countries and similar comparative advantages in production. ASEAN remains an important host for FDI from these countries, even if its relative share has generally been on the

**Table  5.7**
**FDI  (Stock)  from  the  NIEs  (percentage  distribution)**

|  | Korea[*] | | Taiwan[**] | | Hong Kong[§] | | Singapore[§§] | |
|---|---|---|---|---|---|---|---|---|
|  | 1980 | 1988 | 1980 | 1988 | 1884 | 1989 | 1981 | 1989 |
| Developed | | | | | | | | |
| Countries | 32 | 55 | 57 | 71 | 16 | 12 | 9 | 21 |
| Japan | 7 | 3 | .. | .. | 3 | 2 | 0 | 1 |
| Developing | | | | | | | | |
| Countries | 68 | 45 | 43 | 29 | 84 | 88 | 91 | 79 |
| China | .. | .. | .. | .. | 36 | 59 | 0 | 2 |
| Korea | n.a. | n.a | .. | .. | 1 | 1 | 0 | 1 |
| Taiwan | .. | .. | n.a. | n.a. | .. | .. | 1 | 3 |
| Hong Kong | 3 | 1 | .. | .. | n.a | n.a | 11 | 20 |
| Singapore | 1 | 0 | 7 | 3 | .. | .. | 2 | 2 |
| Indonesia | 20 | 17 | 9 | 6 | 22 | 13 | 2 | 2 |
| Malaysia | 0 | 3 | 0 | 3 | 9 | 3 | 60 | 33 |
| Philippines | 1 | 0 | 10 | 8 | 2 | 1 | 1 | 1 |
| Thailand | .. | .. | 5 | 6 | 3 | 2 | 1 | 1 |
| Total | 100 | 100 | 100 | 100 | 100 | 100 | 100 | 100 |
| Amount  (US$ billion,  in 1989 prices) | 0.233 | 1.076 | 0.147 | 0.721 | 7.216 | 13.94 | 1.053 | 1.510 |

* Cumulative approved outflows minus capital withdrawals since 1968.
** Cumulative approved outflows since 1959.
§ Based on host country data.
§§ Value of paid-up shares for affiliates, amount due to parent company for branches.
n.a. = not applicable; .. = not available
*Sources:* United Nations 1992b;  Government of Singapore, *Singapore's Investment Abroad 1976–1989* (1991).

decline. In most cases the absolute values of the investments have increased, though. Indonesia, in particular, is an important host country.

## FDI BY ASEAN COUNTRIES AND CHINA

The data on outward FDI from the ASEAN countries is in most cases rather poor. In order to get some idea of the magnitudes and distribution we have to resort to host country figures for all countries except Thailand. (Singapore was, of course, dealt with in connection with the NIEs and will not be commented on here.) The figures given in Table 5.8 are in U.S. dollars, not in percentages, since we do not have any figures on the total FDI of these countries.

The lack of a total amount of investment and the missing data make it hard to draw far-reaching conclusions from Table 5.8. No clear patterns seem to emerge, except that the NIEs seem to be major hosts to ASEAN FDI in the cases where data availability is sufficient to permit any conclusions to be drawn. The most

**Table 5.8**
**FDI Stocks by the ASEAN Countries (excluding Brunei, Singapore, and Vietnam) (US$ millions)**

| Investor<br>Host Country | Indonesia<br>1988 | Malaysia<br>1988 | Philippines<br>1989 | Thailand<br>1988 |
|---|---|---|---|---|
| Korea | .. | .. | .. | 0 |
| Taiwan | .. | .. | 272 | 0 |
| Hong Kong | .. | 4 | 44 | 105 |
| Singapore | .. | .. | .. | 32 |
| China | 3 | 10 | 67 | 2 |
| Indonesia | n.a. | 46 | 13 | 20 |
| Malaysia | .. | n.a | 42 | 0 |
| Philippines | .. | 7 | n.a. | 0 |
| Thailand | 4 | 21 | 1 | n.a. |

*Note:* .. = not available, n.a. = not applicable.
*Source:* United Nations 1992.

important information in the table is, however, that the outward FDI of the ASEAN countries apparently still is quite small, compared to those of Japan and the NIEs. The Philippine investment in Taiwan and the Thai investment in Hong Kong are the two major concentrations of ASEAN capital that can be accounted for. There is no way to know what exactly might hide behind the missing entries. Some, although not quite comparable, figures are given in Chia (1993). According to that information, the significance of intra-ASEAN investment is in most cases rather small. There was, however, a considerable amount of Malaysian and Indonesian investment in Singapore (S$ 1.3 billion and S$ 174 million, respectively, in 1987), while the corresponding figures for the other ASEAN countries are much smaller.

During the very last years there has been considerable investment from Southeast Asia to China, frequently by overseas Chinese. This surge in activity can be explained to a great extent by the greatly improved political relations between China and Southeast Asia. (Most of these recent flows are not yet included in the figures in Table 5.8.) Some of this investment evidently goes via Hong Kong—and is thus recorded as Hong Kong investment—due to the greater familiarity of Hong Kong companies with the Chinese market (*Asian Business*, April 1993).

Table 5.9 presents China's FDI. While the figures available are quite detailed, the official exchange rate may not reflect the value of the investment quite adequately due to the inconvertibility of the renmimbi. If anything, the figures can be assumed to be somewhat inflated. Table 5.9 tells us that China's FDI is significant, but that the country, like Korea and Taiwan, has concentrated its investment in developed countries. Half of the rest has been invested in Hong Kong. Unfortunately, the figures for China are rather old and do not necessarily tell much about the current situation.

**Table  5.9**
**China's  FDI,  1987  (US$  millions)**

|  | US$ | % of Total |
|---|---|---|
| Developed Countries | 311 | 67 |
| Japan | 6 | 1 |
| Developing Countries | 155 | 33 |
| Korea | — | — |
| Taiwan | — | — |
| Hong Kong | 74 | 16 |
| Singapore | 5 | 1 |
| Indonesia | .. | .. |
| Malaysia | 0 | 0 |
| Philippines | 4 | 1 |
| Thailand | 1 | 0 |
| Total | 466 | 100 |

*Notes:* .. = not available; — = nil.
*Source:* United Nations 1992b.

## THE  INDUSTRIAL  PATTERN  OF  FDI

In the early days, in the 1960s, Japanese investments were to a considerable extent made in the primary sector. Since then there has been a shift, first toward manufacturing, later toward services. The primary (resource) sector now stands for only 10 percent (Hill 1990). In Malaysia, for example, three "waves" of Japanese investment can be distinguished, according to Ariff (1991: 114). In the early 1970s, light industry dominated; in the early 1980s, construction-related activities came to the fore; and the third wave from the latter part of the 1980s on is largely made up of electronics enterprises. Smaller firms are well represented in the last wave, indicating that the manufacturing of electronic components, computer peripherals, and so on is now becoming increasingly unprofitable in Japan. There is, as a general observation, some reason to assume that the FDI of the future, and especially that emanating from the developed countries, will be more technically advanced than before. This in turn means that the investors will have to be more choosy than before when the host countries are selected. The level of human skills will be particularly important, as will also be an adequate infrastructure (cf. UNIDO 1990: ix).[18]

A characteristic of recent Japanese FDI flows is the very high share of service industries; for 1980–84, 61 percent, and for 1985–89, 73 percent. In 1989, for example, investment in the secondary sector was only about one-fourth of total Japanese FDI. The primary sector has declined strongly in a relative sense, even if the investment stock is still growing in absolute terms. The available opportunities here are quite heavily restricted by the host countries' conditions for foreign ownership in the primary sector (Rana 1988: 12; United Nations 1991: 17).

Recent figures on the Japanese investment stock (Drysdale 1992) give the following rough sectoral distribution: agriculture and mining, 5.7 percent;

manufacturing, 26.7 percent; banking and insurance, 19.9 percent; real estate, 15.5 percent; and other services, 32.2 percent. Hence the tertiary sector now stands for somewhat over two-thirds of the total investment in stock terms. The share of investments in service is lower in Asia than for Japanese FDIs taken together, though. Estimates for the late 1980s indicate that the share of the service sector in Asia was then about 50 percent. The Japanese investment in Asia is to a greater extent in industrial production than its overall investment. Even in Asia, the share of manufacturing has been on the decline, however, during the last couple of decades, falling from 44 percent in 1978 to 38 percent in 1988 (Urata 1991: 180). In Asia as a whole, the most important Japanese manufacturing FDIs concern the electrical and electronics industry and the automotive industry, which make up 36 and 14 percent of the total turnover of the Japanese affiliates (United Nations 1991: 22).

Table 5.10 (for which data for China could not be obtained) shows, as expected, a relatively high share of resource-oriented investment in ASEAN (Singapore excluded), while the share is lower for the resource-poor NIEs. Malaysia is something of an exception here, since the country has a relatively low share of Japanese FDI in the resource sector, in spite of being very resource abundant. For the technology and human capital intensive industries (comprising chemicals, general machinery, electric machinery, and transport equipment), the NIEs have, as a rule, a much higher share than ASEAN. Hong Kong is an exception, with a very high share in unskilled labor-intensive industries (predominantly textiles) and a low share in more sophisticated industries.[19] The semi-NIE character of Malaysia is discernible here, the country having a share of technology-intensive investment similar to that of the traditional NIEs.

Figure 5.2 depicts the FDI of the NIEs, ASEAN, and China according to a rough classification into primary, secondary, and tertiary sectors. Unfortunately, it is not possible here to distinguish between intra- and extraregional investment. Hence we do not know exactly whether the industrial pattern of intraregional investment is similar to that of total investment, even if there is some evidence that intraregional manufacturing investment is more labor intensive than FDI as a whole. (Countries lacking statistics on outward investment are left out.)

The FDI of the NIEs is in general concentrated in the manufacturing sector (except for Korea, which has significant investments also in the primary sector, reflecting earlier regulations of FDI and the country's lack of natural resources), particularly electrical and electronic products, textile and apparel, wood products, and "other" manufacturing (e.g., toys); especially labor-intensive parts of production are located in other countries in the region (United Nations 1992b: 30). Taiwan is the only NIE where we have reasonably recent stock data on the industry breakdown of FDI in manufacturing. These figures show that the bulk (80 percent) of this country's FDI in manufacturing is in the technology and human capital-intensive industries.[20] However, it should be remembered that about 70 percent of Taiwan's FDI goes to developed countries. According to Chen (1993), the high-technology based Asian investments are made predominantly in developed countries.

In the case of ASEAN, only figures from Malaysia and Thailand are available. Interestingly enough, both countries have a strong emphasis on the service sector. In the case of Malaysia, the data does not allow us to draw further

**Table 5.10**
**Japan's FDI Stock in Manufacturing, 1988, according to Country and Type of Industry** * **(percentages)**

|  | Agricultural Resource-Intensive | Mineral Resource-Intensive | Unskilled Labour-Intensive | Technology and Human Capital Intensive |
|---|---|---|---|---|
| Developing Asia | 4 | 18 | 22 | 55 |
| Korea | 5 | 7 | 21 | 66 |
| Taiwan | 2 | 9 | 23 | 66 |
| Hong Kong | 11 | 5 | 45 | 39 |
| Singapore | 2 | 5 | 14 | 80 |
| Indonesia | 2 | 48 | 27 | 23 |
| Malaysia | 3 | 14 | 17 | 66 |
| Philippines | 11 | 17 | 13 | 59 |
| Thailand | 7 | 13 | 27 | 54 |

* The classification in Ariff (1991: 199–200) is used, except that technology and human capital-
    intensive industries are aggregated. The food industry is classified as agricultural
    resource-intensive, the metals (ferrous and nonferrous) industry as mineral resource-
    intensive, textiles and "other" industries as unskilled labor-intensive, and chemicals,
    machinery, transport equipment, and paper and pulp as technology and human capital-
    intensive.
*Source*: Urata 1991: 180–181.


**Figure 5.2**
**Sectoral Distribution of FDI of Selected East Asian Countries**

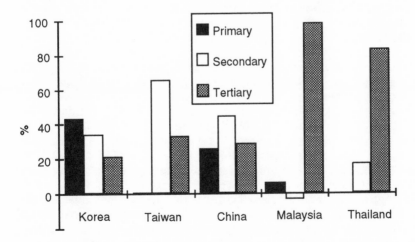

*Note:* The data are for the late 1980s, but exact year varies for different countries.
*Source:* United Nations 1992b.

conclusions, even if the hospitality business is probably important here, while the Thai investment is largely in the banking sector. Details on the secondary sector are available only for Thailand. These figures show that more than three-fourths of Thai FDI are in resource-intensive industries, while the rest is almost completely in labor-intensive activities.

The Chinese investment is relatively evenly distributed over the three main sectors. The country seems to invest heavily in resource-intensive industries, but also displays large shares in technology and human capital-intensive industries. In this case, however, 41 percent of the investments in the secondary sector was unallocated, which makes it well nigh impossible to draw conclusions on whether the distribution overall follows that of the investment that can be assigned to a certain category.

## DEVELOPMENT AID

The issue of development aid (usually referred to as Official Development Assistance, ODA) is best taken up in the context of investment, since, like investment, aid transfers resources—tangible and intangible—from a source to a recipient. Moreover, aid may be used strategically by a donor country to prepare the ground for direct investments through improving infrastructure and so on. Unlike FDI, aid is administered and its funding is raised by government institutions. Hence it is almost inevitable that political considerations have a bearing on the exact nature of aid supplied and what countries are to be recipients. Except in the case of emergency aid, the donor usually expects to have something to gain from aid, too, be it in terms of economic, political, security, or cultural benefits. Aid may also be tied to conditions regarding democracy, human rights, environmental protection and so on, which are often rather unprecise concepts and thus subject to the discretion of the donor (Anwar 1995). In the case of multilateral aid, conditions as regards macroeconomic management are attached as a matter of routine.

Japan is today the world's leading donor of development aid, the main part of which goes to the East Asian region. About half of the Japanese bilateral ODA to Asia goes to ASEAN, while China is the biggest single recipient country. In ASEAN, the Japanese aid is of paramount importance, as illustrated by the magnitude of that aid as related to total aid. In 1987, for instance, Indonesia received 70 percent of its aid from Japan, while the corresponding figures for the other ASEAN countries are: Thailand, 74 percent; the Philippines, 57 percent; and Malaysia, 45 percent (Grosser and Bridges 1990). Much of Japanese ODA—especially the grants—is tied to procurement of Japanese goods and services, which tends to strengthen the ties between donor and recipient. On the other hand, the grant element in Japanese aid seems to have fallen recently, and the loans are usually not tied to purchases of Japanese goods. In fact, the ratio of tied aid, in the case of Japan, is one of the lowest of all donor countries (Kohama 1995). Even without formally tying aid, however, part will easily flow back to the donor. This is especially the case when project aid is concerned, since that aid is usually initiated by the recipient which gives the donor country a possibility to customize a proposal using domestic inputs (Rix 1989/90; Cronin 1992: 38, 43; Koppel and Plummer 1989).

Due to the lack of personnel and, partly because of this, a somewhat unclear ODA agenda[21], the Japanese tend to rely on aid proposals submitted by prospective recipients. In that case Japanese companies in the recipient countries are often the agents that initiate projects (Lincoln 1990: 34). Some caution is warranted, however, as to maintaining that this would be a typically Japanese trait. For some arguments in favor of the Japanese type of foreign aid, see Kohama and Teranishi (1992) and Kohama (1995). They explain the latter "model" with the alleged Japanese emphasis on long-run growth, taking account of the fact that the typical Japanese view on economic development is much less generalizing than the standard Western one. In that case it makes sense to let the development projects emanate from the recipient countries themselves. Kohama (1995) also points out that the de facto policy of Japan is usually based on this country's own earlier experiences of economic development.

There seems to be a distinctly regional approach by leading officials in Japan, an allegation that may be supported to some extent by a quotation from a speech of the then Prime Minister of Japan, Toshiki Kaifu (cf. also Koppel and Plummer 1989):

Japan will, for example, continue to seek to expand imports from the countries of the region and promote greater investment in and technology transfer to these countries, in line with the maturity of their trade structure and their stages of development. And as the necessary complement to this effort, I hope that the host countries will make an even greater effort to create a climate receptive to Japanese investment and technology transfer.(Kaifu 1991)

This quotation neatly summarizes the role of aid in the context of the "Flying Geese" model, when that model is interpreted as a normative one.

The significance of development assistance in the context of changing economic interdependence is, to a considerable degree, indirect. Nevertheless, Japanese foreign aid is a central device for the country to influence the economic restructuring in the Asia-Pacific region, and at the same time to secure benefits for the Japanese economy. It is a common view that Japan has been behaving "strategically" in the realm of ODA, in the sense that these efforts have been made in a way that has been favorable to Japanese commercial interests (cf. Dobson 1993: 20). The country also has the possibility of supporting its aid policy through its influence on multilateral agencies, especially the Asian Development Bank.

As touched on above, the most straightforward effects of aid are likely to emanate from investments in heavy infrastructure, which are the predominant object for Japanese ODA. Such investments are, on the one hand, a prerequisite for any significant industrialization. On the other hand, investment in infrastructure may well be carried out by a donor that primarily is concerned about the interests of the economy of its own country, hence facilitating FDI from that country. More directly, Japanese companies can readily take advantage of infrastructural projects in the form of contracts for Japanese engineering and construction companies (Cronin 1992: 18). While this may not necessarily be a negative trait as such, it is almost certain to be a second-best solution to the

**Table   5.11**
**Bilateral  ODA  Flows  from  Japan,  1990,  US$  millions**

| Region | US$ millions | Percentage |
|---|---|---|
| Asia | 4117 | 59.3 |
|     Northeast Asia | 835 | 12.0 |
|     Southeast Asia | 2379 | 34.3 |
|     ASEAN * | 2299 | 33.1 |
|     Southwest Asia ** | 898 | 12.9 |
|     Unspecified | 4 | 0.0 |
| Middle East | 705 | 10.2 |
| Africa | 792 | 11.4 |
| Central and South America | 561 | 8.1 |
| Oceania | 14 | 1.6 |
| Europe | 158 | 2.3 |
| Unallocable | 494 | 7.1 |
| Total | 6940 | 100.0 |

* Vietnam not included.
** In Japan this term stands for South Asia.
*Source*: Cronin 1992: 17

extent that the aid is actually tied to deliveries from the donor country. Japanese aid has frequently been criticized for allegedly favoring Japanese interests before those of the recipient, and creating an economic zone in Asia under Japanese leadership. On the other hand, domestic coordination of the aid effort seems rather poorly developed (cf. Koppel and Plummer 1989; Rix 1989/90). This may be a temporary phenomenon. The rapid increase in the sums allocated for ODA may simply have outrun the administrative capability of the relevant agencies in Japan.

Japan is of course not the only donor country where the phenomenon of aid for the sake of the donor's benefit has been apparent. In any case, the aid often seems to be targeted at development complementary to that of the Japanese economy (cf. Cronin 1992: 40). It may be noted that the dramatic increase in Japan's foreign aid coincided with the explosion of FDI, which in turn must have been a consequence of the appreciation of the yen since the mid-1980s (cf. Koppel and Plummer 1989). This, if anything, lends more credibility to the idea that the two are coordinated. As a matter of fact, the bilateral official development aid flows from Japan are of roughly the same magnitude as the FDI. Table 5.11 gives an overview of the situation in 1990.

The role of the NIEs as donors on a greater scale cannot be evaluated well at this moment, since these countries have become net donors very recently. According to some sources, there are certain signs of a pattern similar to the alleged Japanese one, which tends to see aid in the context of the economic interest of the donor country (cf. Grosser and Bridges 1990; Koppel and Plummer 1989). Such a judgment must be looked upon with a good deal of caution, though. In the case of Singapore, training awards and assistance seem to play a major role. Under the Singapore Cooperation Programme, which was set up only in 1992, the country sponsors more than 2,000 officials from more than eighty different countries participating in courses covering widely different areas, such as civil aviation, medicine and information technology (*Singapore*, May/June 1993).

## CONCLUSIONS

A complicated network of transnational business is now developing in East Asia. To a great extent, this network is being formed by Asian companies, taking advantage of both rapidly growing markets and the opportunity to diversify production geographically in order to utilize different comparative advantages in different countries and to establish export platforms from which the region as well as other markets can be catered to. These activities have often been supported by aid-financed infrastructural development, above all with the support of Japanese ODA. Although Japan is still the most important intraregional investor, the NIEs are also very significant actors by now—in fact, in a relative sense they are, as a group, much more active investors than Japan. Also ASEAN (minus Singapore) and China are not negligible foreign direct investors in the region, although their investments so far are typically rather small compared to those of Japan and the NIEs.

Hence, even in the absence of formal market integration, a considerable degree of de facto integration and incentives to enhance cooperation further in the region are now developing. As a matter of fact, initiatives recently taken to bring about economic integration and cooperation in the region rather appear to be propelled by the actual events instead of being the reason for them. The foreign trade regime has been liberalized greatly during the last couple of decades, a process that is still going on. The ASEAN Free Trade Area (AFTA), now taking shape, should provide new incentives for FDI, however. Meanwhile "growth triangles," allowing investors a flexible framework to cross national borders in a subregional context, is a way, albeit apparently a second-best one, to improve the external environment for FDI.

## NOTES

1. The region covered in this chapter is here defined operationally as Japan, China, South Korea, Taiwan, Hong Kong and five ASEAN countries (Malaysia, Indonesia, the Philippines, Singapore, and Thailand). Brunei and Myanmar (Burma), as well as the "Indochinese" countries of Vietnam, Laos, and Cambodia, had to be excluded due to a lack of data. Of these, Brunei is a significant investor, but since its investment is mainly administered through foreign agencies, direct investment is most probably not very significant.

2. Even if and when international standards are arrived at, measurement of the real value of FDI will inevitably be difficult and controversial, due to the immaterial parts of the investment, consisting primarily of technology, management, and market access. It is quite conceivable that these immaterial parts are even more important than the sheer capital injection, especially as FDI seems to be associated with the existence of knowledge-based assets (cf. Markusen 1991: 15, 30).

3. Two common definitions exist. IMF defines FDI as investment made to acquire lasting interest in enterprises operating outside of the economy of the investor. Further, the direct investor's purpose is to gain an effective voice in the management of the enterprise. OECD defines FDI as an enterprise in which a single investor holds 10 percent or more of the ordinary shares or voting power (unless it can be shown that the 10 percent ownership does not allow the investor an effective voice in the management) or owns less than 10 percent of the ordinary shares or voting power, but still maintains an effective voice in management (United Nations 1992b: 39). Discrepancies between countries may be caused either by different interpretations of these rules or because different data bases are used (e.g., balance of payments data, approved investment, implemented investment, or company assets). See, for example, Rana (1988) for a comparison of IMF and OECD data.

4. An interesting attempt to do this for the case of Japan is reported in Dobson (1993: ch. 6). She found some support for Dunning's eclectic theory of FDI (cf. e.g. Dunning 1980).

5. According to established custom, the NIE category includes Hong Kong, Korea, Singapore, and Taiwan. The classification is not intended to convey the view of the author on whether these economies are "developed" or not.

6. High income economies like Singapore and Hong Kong are included in this category, partly because of the UN's classification standards, partly because such a classification serves the purpose of this study, separating Japan from the other East Asian countries. According to the UN classification, areas classified as "developed" comprise Western Europe (except Yugoslavia and Malta), North America, and, additionally, Australia, Israel, Japan, New Zealand, South Africa, and Turkey. Hence in Asia all countries other than Israel and Japan are classified as "developing" (United Nations 1992b: 38).

7. Much of the funds originate in Hong Kong.

8. The latter argument has lately been relevant for the NIEs, as they have been deprived of their LDC status as far as the GSP treatment in the United States is concerned.

9. Summaries of current policies toward FDI of the countries in the Asia-Pacific region are provided by the *Asian Business* magazine, and United Nations 1992b: 3–7. See also Phongpaichit (1990: 69–88) for a survey of the ASEAN countries.

10. The figure is for all Asia, but only the East Asian countries are of any significance here. The estimate does not contain non-OECD source countries, and is thus too small, but the argument remains valid.

11. Taiwan and Korea were the first important targets particularly because the Japanese language was widely spoken in these countries (Ichimura 1988: 38).

12. Liberalization in Taiwan during the 1980s has facilitated FDI greatly, while Korea started relaxing its restrictions on FDI in 1984 (even if the reality is still one of less openness than the official policy indicates; see Cheeseman 1992). A visible increase in the level of FDI has been the consequence. The industry of Taiwan is much less capital intensive than its Korean counterpart, which may explain the relatively modest FDI in spite of a more open regime (cf. Hill 1990).

13. Active discrimination against Korean goods seems to have marred the investment climate even further (cf. Cronin 1992: 29).

14. Multinational companies are a very important part of Singapore's economy, and some of the FDI originating in the republic is made by such enterprises rather than by Singaporean companies (see UNIDO 1990: 21).

15. The figure was given in March 1993 (Baum 1993).

16. According to Ariff (1991: 116), much of the Taiwanese FDI may in fact be Malaysian Chinese capital "recycled" via Taiwan in order to take advantage of the

investment incentives and to beat the NEP-related regulations on domestic firms (cf. also Cronin 1992: 25). No hard evidence of this is available, though.

17. The relatively small figure for Korean FDI in Asia is "explained" partly by the fact that the country invests more outside Asia and partly by its industrial structure. The latter is dominated by very big conglomerates ("chaebol") which are active in a wide range of industries and which are in a position to upgrade their production structure as an alternative to relocating to cheaper sites of production (cf. UNIDO 1990: 21). A clear increase in the role of small and medium-size firms in Korean FDI is now discernible, however. In 1989, for example, smaller firms stood for about 10 percent of total Korean FDI in terms of value. As a percentage of the total number of investments they were about one-third (Waitt 1993).

18. At a general level, it has been found that skill intensity of a firm is positively related to overseas investment activity. This seems to imply that it is often the technically advanced firms that seek to localize the less advanced part of their production to sites with a more advantageous level of production costs. (The most advanced firms are likely to be the ones with the best capability to organize such a geographical decentralization, too.) The potential provided by FDI may be greater because of this than the type of production on the spot would suggest (cf. United Nations 1992a: 9).

19. This reflects the still very "light" character of Hong Kong manufacturing. (Hong Kong today is largely a service economy, with much of its manufacturing located on the mainland Chinese side of the border. The growth of the service sector can to a great extent be explained by the demand generated by the opening up of the Chinese economy; Chen 1993.)

20. The figures must be interpreted with caution. For instance, we classified the category "electrical equipment" as technology-intensive, but parts of that industry are quite labor-intensive.

21. Kohama (1995) explains that although the explicit formulation of ODA policy in Japan is rather unspecific, four general principles tend to be adhered to in practice: a low share of grants, emphasis on project financing, relying on requests by recipients, and the principle of help to self-help.

# 6

## Organization of Economic Cooperation in the Asia-Pacific Region

### INTRODUCTION

Formalized economic arrangements are not, of course, forged between countries at a similar level of development only. Nevertheless, in order to overcome protectionism, declining terms-of-trade, and too small domestic markets, many less developed countries over the years have resorted to regional cooperation with other LDCs, particularly because such a strategy was explicitly recommended by early development economists (see, e.g., Hunt 1989: ch. 5). Some of the past and present efforts at cooperation in East Asia should be understood against that background. Additionally, perceived political advantages have frequently been a reason why international organizations have been formed. The general impression of the outcome of such schemes in the real world is, however, rather gloomy, particularly from the economic point of view but often from the political point of view as well. Many regional economic organizations have been established, with high hopes, but few of them can, by any standards, be regarded as a success. Sometimes the failures have been fairly easy to predict with the aid of some economic theory (see, for instance, Blomqvist and Lindholm 1992).

As the preceding chapters have clearly shown, de facto economic integration—in the sense that the economies of the region are becoming more and more intertwined—is already well under way in East Asia. It is inevitable that this contributes to increasing the pressure toward formalized cooperation in the region, as increasing interdependence holds potential for both mutual gains and conflicts. A way of managing these issues thus has to be envisaged. There are also other good reasons for economic cooperation, as will be argued shortly.

This chapter elaborates on the organizational aspect of the emerging interdependence in the region. The scope is widened in order to take the larger Asia-Pacific region into account, not just East Asia, because many emerging attempts at cooperation have encompassed parts of the eastern Pacific region as well. In fact, the Pacific Rim has often been analyzed as one region, as demonstrated, for example, by the catchword "Pacific Century," alluding to the promising future of this part of the world. We will not consider organizations without East Asian membership, though, despite the fact that some of them may be indirectly relevant for East Asia, such as the North American Free Trade Area (NAFTA).

## THEORETICAL ASPECTS ON ECONOMIC COOPERATION BETWEEN LDCs

The distinction between the concepts of integration and economic cooperation is not always very sharp in the literature, but the terms are often used interchangeably. In this chapter, integration—as a policy[1]—denotes the absence or abolition of discrimination between domestic and foreign goods, services, and factors of production (cf. Balassa 1988: 43; Robson 1984: 1). Cooperation is a broader concept involving mutual adjustment of policies in a certain area. The term can denote any form of agreement, achieved through formal or tacit bargaining between states, aimed at enhancing the common interests of the parties involved, starting from occasional consultation, and ending in complete policy coordination (Cohen 1993). According to this definition, all international organizations and agreements, including those aimed at integration, can be regarded as cooperation.

Even if the term *economic integration* is more precise than *cooperation,* it can stand for many different levels of ambition, covering anything from preferential trade relations in specific products between two countries to a complete merger of the economies. The common purpose of all forms of integration is to eliminate barriers to trade and/or factor movements between the member countries, while some degree of protection against third countries is maintained. This chapter will not deal with more advanced forms of integration—common markets and economic unions—since these are somewhat unrealistic alternatives in the Asia-Pacific region of today.

The benefits of international cooperation emerge from joint production of supranational public (or quasi-public) goods or control of international external effects. In general, economic exchange between countries benefits from institutions complementary to production of private goods. Many such institutions can be interpreted as producing public goods. Public goods are freely available to all—once they are produced—so they would not be produced by private initiative. A special type of public goods are external effects, which are positive or negative spillover effects from one economic activity to another. They are not traded in markets because of the difficulties to assign property rights to them (Richardson 1993), which again partly is a consequence of the difficulty of measuring them but also a consequence of their character as public goods. Typical international public goods are international law and order (defense, trading regime, and harmonization of industrial standards, certification and testing).[2] Externalities are common, especially in the fields of environmental effects, education, and health care. Cooperation in the field of externalities or public goods is in many cases desirable from an efficiency point of view, but often encounters obstacles due to conflicts about the distribution of costs and benefits between the participants or vested interests for a single country or pressure group. The free rider problem—the benefits accrue also to nonparticipating countries—is likely to be present in most cases as well.

It may be noted that cooperation—even if it is presented as economic cooperation—has emerged not only from purely economic factors but from political and security considerations as well. It is very hard in practice to draw the line between organizations with an economic purpose and those with a political purpose. The reason is, of course, that political stability and security is a *sine qua non* for economic development. Apart from international conflicts, internal subversion has frequently been a threat to economic development and may be more effectively addressed by means of international cooperation.

International cooperation can, in principle, take place on an ad hoc basis. This is also frequently how it is pursued. However, even if international cooperation would be clearly advantageous, it may in many cases be difficult, or cost too much, to coordinate the actions of sovereign nations on an ad hoc basis. That is why it may be optimal for the countries involved to form an organization or make agreements where the rules of the cooperative effort are stated (Frey 1991: 10). This tends to save transaction costs which usually are higher in intercountry than in intracountry transactions, due to language problems, lack of information on local customs, legislation and so on (Harris 1993). For example, an international or regional trading regime can be regarded as a public good, complementary to foreign trade in that the latter would be seriously impaired in the absence of this good (Frey 1991: 9). Despite this, no single country can achieve an orderly trading system on its own, and a case-by-case approach is hardly feasible either. Another case in point is externalities extending across national borders. Environmental effects of economic activities are a typical case, the consequences of drug trafficking another. Among developing countries, regional cooperation has sometimes been perceived as an instrument for influencing global organizations, such as the World Bank and GATT. Finally, a multinational organization could also be used as an instrument for fending off demands by domestic special interest groups.

The free rider problem relates to the difficulties of forming and preserving a stable organization; the single member may have an incentive not to join the organization and still reap the benefits or to disobey the rules, provided everyone else adheres to them. International commodity cartels are a well-known case in point. In a less extreme case, the contribution of a country to a common budget may not be proportional to its gains, because the individual member may want to stop contributing to the production costs before the optimal production for the group as a whole is reached (Olson and Zeckhauser 1966). The free rider problem indicates that organizations involving a small group of countries are more feasible than those that involve numerous countries (Frey 1991: 13) since it is easier to administer sanctions in a small group. The size of a grouping is also often limited by the tendency of administration costs to rise more than proportionally with each new member, while the additional benefits for the earlier members may well be falling (Fratianni and Pattison 1982).

The problem with evaluating the performance of a supranational organization is that its "output" is usually vaguely defined and difficult to measure (cf. Frey

1984: 151; Frey and Gygi 1991: 60–61). Partly for that reason, partly because of a lack of incentives to monitor its performance, the administrative procedures of an international organization, and the bureaucracy, which has an interest of its own in expanding the administration, are hard to control. This may impose a gradually increasing deadweight loss to be deduced from the "output" of the organization. How great the net gain is, and how it is distributed between the member countries, are very hard to assess, considering these general problems.

Finally, a problem encountered by cooperating countries is political differences between and within the nations. Factors such as historical, cultural, and geographical preconditions, regional political interactions, and economic development are likely to be instrumental for the outcome of cooperation efforts since a favorable combination of such factors tends to lower the obstacles to reaching an agreement. Many LDCs are still in the process of finding their national identity; therefore it is common that developing nations will guard strongly against any sacrifice of their newly won sovereignty, and borders will consequently gain in importance (Langhammer and Hiemenz 1990: 14).

In East Asia there used to be considerable resistance to cooperation, at least cooperation encompassing the whole Asia-Pacific region. Some of this resistance is still discernible. The reasons varied from fear of domination by the United States or Japan, which is still resented in many East Asian countries due to wartime events, skepticism about its usefulness, and concerns about effects on already established subregional cooperation (especially in the case of the Association of Southeast Asian Nations). Even if this has partly changed now, with increasing interdependence and the recognition that problems caused by interdependence have to be addressed, many countries are still reluctant. As noted by Harris (1994), the policy implications of increasing interdependence are not obvious and views on how problems should be addressed are rather different.

It is usually assumed that an international organization functions according to the "national interest" of the members, that is, sees to the best interest of the whole entity. (For a summary of the traditional arguments in favor of international organizations, see Vaubel 1991: 28–31.) The situation is complicated, however, by the fact that, at the end of the day, individuals make the decisions, not nations. According to the so-called public choice school, there is no such thing as "national interest," but the term is used by politicians and bureaucrats as a rhetorical device for defending their personal interest (cf. Frey and Gygi 1991: 65). (Part of that interest may, of course, be what they perceive as a national interest.) Thus it may be maintained that a country will not join an organization if the key decision makers in that country do not have anything to gain from membership. For instance, a government would not subscribe to an agreement that would be likely to lead to its being voted out of office. In many developing countries, particularly if the economy has been very sheltered, there are strong alliances between industrialists and politicians. In such cases the alleged national interest may in reality be the interest of a powerful lobby.

No matter what the benefits for the whole prospective grouping may be, the decision to join an organization is an outcome of the interest of the single participating country—whatever that may imply—not the benefits of the grouping as a whole. Hence, even if an organization would be beneficial from the point of view of all members, taken together, it may not be formed (or survive) if the single members are not convinced about the gains accruing to themselves.

## ECONOMIC INTEGRATION BETWEEN DEVELOPING COUNTRIES

The theoretical discussion on economic integration among LDCs emerged in the early 1950s as a result of the so-called Latin American structuralist paradigm on the one hand, and the classical customs union theory on the other. The early structuralism provided arguments based on the conviction that the prevailing world trade system inherently tends to exploit the LDCs and perpetuate their poverty. The prospects for exports of primary goods were considered unfavorable, and the import barriers in the more developed countries allegedly prevented exports of manufactured goods. Consequently, industrialization through import substitution and—because of small local markets—regional economic integration appeared to be attractive policy options for many LDCs. Thus the LDCs were encouraged to promote development through import substitution and closer regional cooperation (cf. Johnson 1967: 25–32; Hunt 1989: 141–143). This view was endorsed by UNCTAD (United Nations Conference on Trade and Development) in 1964 (cf., e.g., Suriyamongkol 1988: 50).

In recent years the "fallacy of composition" argument has provided some additional support for this idea. According to this notion, it may be possible for some countries to employ successfully an outward-oriented development strategy, but it would not be possible for all because the increasing supply of exports would cause the prices to collapse or evoke protectionist countermeasures from the developed countries. Finally, the rapid moves toward integration in Europe and North America during recent years have clearly been inspiring to new efforts also in other parts of the world (cf., e.g., Lee 1991; *Straits Times*, January 28, 1992).

Viner (1950), followed by Meade (1955) and Lipsey (1957, 1960), pioneered the study of comparative static effects of a customs union on trade flows, resource allocation, and welfare. Viner showed that the formation of a customs union combines elements of free trade with elements of protection, which may result in either positive or negative net welfare effects. He minted the now standard concepts of trade creation and trade diversion to distinguish between the positive and negative effects (from a welfare point of view) of a customs union. Trade creation refers to the replacement of higher-cost domestic production by lower-cost imports from partner countries, while trade diversion implies the replacement of lower-cost imports from third countries by higher-cost imports from member countries, both effects emerging as a result of the elimination of tariffs in intraregional trade. The net welfare result of a customs union, then, according to his view, depends on which effect will dominate. [3]

The traditional static effects may, however, account for only part of the consequences of economic integration. The implicit assumption of full employment that is implicitly part of the neoclassical analytical framework may not hold, of course, so we may obtain an additional effect through the customs union's effect on resource utilization. Moreover, the dynamic effects of integration are often considered the principal argument in favor of economic integration (see e.g. Balassa 1961: pt. 2; Corden 1972; and El-Agraa and Jones 1981: Ch. 6).

The dynamic effects refer to a number of long-term consequences of free trade arrangements affecting the growth rate of GDP, such as economies of scale, enhanced competition and efficiency, intraindustry specialization, and intensified investment activities. Economic integration may improve efficiency by encouraging competition and specialization among producers in the member countries. Monopolies and oligopolies are no longer protected by national barriers, and the number of potential competitors increases, and that may improve the performance of individual companies and shift resources from less efficient to more efficient production. Competition also provides incentives for increased research activity and faster technological progress (Balassa and Stoutjesdijk 1976: 40; Meier 1989: 428). Finally, there should be a significant reduction of intraregional transaction costs (Reynolds 1992). All these effects may be very significant, especially in the long run. Since, however, the dynamic effects are difficult to analyze rigorously within the framework of traditional economic models, they have been hard to quantify and have aroused widespread debate and controversy even if their significance is widely acknowledged.

The likelihood of a customs union to generate positive welfare effects is greater, the larger the market share of domestic goods and the smaller the share of imported goods from nonmember countries is before establishing the union. The larger the internal market of the customs union is, the more significant is also the potential positive welfare effect. (From this follows, of course, that a market comprising the whole world would be the optimal solution; that is, free trade is the limiting, optimal, case.) Finally, the higher the pre-union tariffs have been, the greater is the possibility of trade creation and welfare gains, and the lower the external tariff is set, the smaller will be the risk of trade diversion.

Differences in production structures among members of a customs union can affect the outcome of the union. A customs union will—perhaps counterintuitively—increase welfare the more competitive the production structures of the member countries are and the more substituting for each other they are (cf., e.g., Robson 1984: 19). Substitutability provides room for both inter- and intraindustrial specialization, which facilitates the exploitation of scale economies. Moreover, for a specific production overlap, potential trade creation is greater the larger the differences in unit costs are in the countries prior to the union (Robson 1984: 19–20).These effects may not come forth in countries with a low level of income, where manufactured products tend to be too basic and standardized for these effects to be important (cf. Akrasanee 1984: 33). Such specialization also inevitably implies that some existing capacity has to be closed down, however, which is bound to cause political difficulties (Lewis 1980). Hence a conflict between general and specific interests may be an obstacle to integration.

One of the most important sources of conflict in the process of integration (and other forms of cooperation as well), particularly among developing countries, is the problem involving intercountry distributional effects. Free trade tends to accentuate inequalities in the process of regional cooperation among developing countries (Lewis 1980; Vaitsos 1978). This is the so-called polarization effect. Differences between partner countries concerning their income and industrialization level will lead to a polarization in favor of the relatively more advanced nations. The less developed a member country is, the smaller will be the comparative static trade effects as well as the dynamic production effects. Particularly low pre-union levels of industrialization and lack of capital act as an obstacle to the realization of dynamic gains. These types of objections have been common in the case of integration in East Asia, whether they have had a rational foundation or not.


## THE REALITY—ECONOMIC ORGANIZATIONS IN ASIA-PACIFIC

As observed, for example, by Lloyd (1994), East Asia is the least regionalized part of the world as far as customs unions and free trade areas are concerned. This is also true for other organizations in the economic realm, despite the fact that the interest in developing closer links between the countries in the East Asian or the larger Asia-Pacific region has been considerable over the years. The concrete results so far have been meager, at least if ASEAN is excluded. Increasing interdependence is likely to lead to more organized cooperation in the future, however.

The relative lack of organizations in the region is not surprising; in fact, there are several good reasons for this state of affairs. To begin with, East Asia was, at the end of World War II, still dominated by colonial and semi-colonial interests not conducive to regional cooperation. East Asia was seldom perceived as a region at all. Neither were the emerging independence movements primarily interested in international cooperation at the time, being occupied by gaining control and developing the fundamental institutions of their own countries. Moreover, the region was full of conflicts, such as disputes over national borders and ethnic cleavages. The cold war, in its turn, imposed a division of the region into two different camps, seriously limiting most forms of cooperation. Hence cooperative schemes have not had much time or scope to develop (cf. Higgott, Leaver, and Ravenhill 1993). One prominent exception was the Institute of Pacific Relations (IPR) which was set up as early as in 1925. The institute was dismantled in 1961 largely because of political sentiments in the United States at the time. Bringing together academics, business people, politicians, and government officials, it fulfilled a role as a well-respected forum of discussion not unlike that of several nongovernmental organizations established much later (Woods 1991).

Only in the 1990s have the preconditions for economic cooperation in the region changed decisively, even if most of the intellectual roots of the present arrangements can be found in the mid-1960s (cf. Harris 1994). Many problems remain, though. The countries in the Asia-Pacific region encompass an extremely heterogeneous group of economies in almost every sense imaginable. Moreover, the rate of change in many of these countries has been very rapid during the last few decades, a fact that may easily cause tensions between countries. Increasing interdependence, while increasing the need for cooperation, is a source of friction as well. To this must be added  complications caused by the delicate political situation in the region where several regimes are considered illegitimate by part of the neighboring countries, with remaining territorial disputes and other conflicts. In order to work, cooperation channels in such cases often have to be of an unofficial character (cf. Elek 1991). In fact, as a result of the end of the cold war, the political situation has become less clear-cut and less predictable than before. It is important to realize, however, that economic cooperation is not carried out only between governments. As observed by Harris (1994), market actors, for example, are important as well.

Much of the early initiatives for cooperation had a background in security concerns in the region as a result of the volatile political situation at the time, but encompassed ideas about technical assistance and other forms of economic cooperation as well. The so-called Colombo Plan of 1950 was one of the first major moves in this direction. The Colombo Plan emphasized mutual technical assistance (Harris 1991). An idea to clone OECD onto the Asia-Pacific region was floated in the late 1970s. The proposed organization, OPTAD (Organization for Pacific Trade, Aid, and Development), turned out to be a non-starter, but the discussion and feasibility study of the issue prepared the ground for subsequent developments, apparently as they took shape in the Pacific Economic Cooperation Conference (PECC), discussed below. As emphasized by Harris (1993), the OECD countries held in common basic socioeconomic foundations, such as a liberal market economy, while the Asia-Pacific countries were far more different among themselves.

The Asian Development Bank was formed in 1966 (Harris 1991) and ASEAN in 1967 (ASEAN was joined by Brunei in 1984 and by Vietnam in 1995 ), after several aborted attempts at forming associations between some or all of the Southeast Asian countries. Like the ADB, some organizations have members from outside the region or are subsidiaries of other international bodies, such as the United Nations Economic and Social Commission for Asia and the Pacific and its predecessor, the Economic Commission for Asia and the Far East (ECAFE), which was founded as early as in 1947. The ADB, besides engaging in providing credits for the development of member countries, also undertakes research, coordination, and planning work. ESCAP (which covers both South and Central Asia and the Pacific except for East Asia), has a secretariat in Bangkok and has been engaged mostly in research and planning activities. Many of these early efforts were conceived to address the paramount problem of the Asia-Pacific region at that time, underdevelopment (Harris 1991).

The most important nongovernmental organizations in the region are the Pacific Economic Cooperation Conference, PAFTAD (Pacific Trade and Development Conference), a body consisting of academics and policy advisers, and PBEC (Pacific Basin Economic Council), which is a business cooperation group (Harris 1991). PECC, founded in 1980, is officially a nongovernmental organization, where the members act in their private capacities.[4] The organization is a tripartite group, having members from the business and academic communities but also from the public sector. PAFTAD and PBEC are members as well. The organization is led by a Standing Committee and since 1990 has a secretariat in Singapore. PECC aims at promoting regional cooperation in the Pacific region. It is involved in, among other things, research in agriculture, fisheries, and human resource development (Union of International

Associations 1995: 1305). PECC is a low-key organization, but its composition makes sure that its standpoints are passed on to the governments.

PAFTAD and PBEC were founded in the late 1960s (Woods 1991) and may be seen as forerunners to PECC. In these organizations, formal bureaucracy is almost nonexistent and the political connections loose, which has been an advantage when dealing with delegates from politically disparate countries. PBEC is made up of national committees of business executives (more than 1,000 companies are represented).[5] Among its objectives can be mentioned relation building between business communities in the region, increased trade and investment in the Pacific, and enhanced economic and social progress in developing countries in the region. The organization also provides advice to governments on development issues in the region (Union of International Associations 1995: 1304). (This approach has allowed, as in PECC, for instance, China, Taiwan and Hong Kong to be members simultaneously.)

PAFTAD, which was originally a gathering to discuss a Japanese proposal on forming a free trade area (PAFTA, see below), is more academically oriented than the other organizations, aiming at promoting discussion on Asian-Pacific economic issues, and related academic policy-oriented research. PAFTAD provides a forum for discussions on current economic developments in the region in the form of annual conferences. The Steering Committee includes members from North America, Asia and Australasia, but participants from other countries are also present on an invitation basis (Union of International Associations 1995: 1306). An International Secretariat is located in Canberra. Even if these groupings are extremely low-key as far as their public appearance is concerned, they have most probably been conducive to subsequent attempts at more high-profile cooperation.

The most recent major proposal in this context, on forming an East Asian Economic Group (EAEG), was mooted by the prime minister of Malaysia, Datuk Seri Dr. Mahathir Mohamad, at a meeting of PECC (Rafidah 1991; Lee 1991). (The name was altered to East Asia Economic Caucus [EAEC] at the meeting of the Economic Ministers of ASEAN in October 1991 in Kuala Lumpur: *New Straits Times*, October 9, 1991.)

EAEC, according to Dr. Mahathir (Okamoto 1995), would counter attempts at forming trade blocs in other parts of the world and offer a common and powerful platform for the East Asian countries in international trade negotiations. The leading idea has been to promote an open international environment, however, not to create another inward-looking bloc (see Harris 1993). EAEC seems to be implicitly based on a notion like the "Flying Geese," in particular as far as the role of Japan as the leader of the flock is concerned. One interpretation is that the main rationale behind the initiative is to connect Japan closer to its Asian neighbors, instead of being more and more involved in the markets of the European Union and the United States.

Whether EAEC will be a significant instrument to that effect remains to be seen. So far the concept has not convinced other East Asian nations, even if they have not wanted to dismiss it downright. The proposal would need at least the unambiguous support of Japan to be of any practical significance, and so far this support has not come forth, presumably due to Japan's own important economic connections to the United States. The reception of the EAEC proposal in other

Asian countries has been ambivalent, too, not least because of the apparent overlap with other similar organizations (Low 1991). Hence, after five years, EAEC remains little more than a proposal with an uncertain future, even if it has been formally accepted as a caucus within Asia-Pacific Economic Cooperation which will be discussed later. Today the most likely fate of the project seems to be a quiet demise when Dr. Mahathir steps down.

In the Asia-Pacific region, ideas on *integration* are of more recent origin. As noted in several connections (see, e.g., Elek 1995), integration in the Asia-Pacific region has been market driven, not driven by institution building and political initiatives. The latter have regularly been more a result of the process than the reason for it. The first significant initiative was a Japanese[6] proposal for a Pacific Free Trade Area (PAFTA), but this proposed organization, which never materialized, was supposed to encompass only the developed countries in the region (Harris 1993). Recently, integration schemes have been initiated by both ASEAN and APEC (Asia-Pacific Economic Cooperation).

ASEAN's role in building up regional cooperative networks is impossible to neglect here, even if ASEAN is a subregional organization by nature. Especially the postministerial conferences, from 1974 on (the institutional basis for ASEAN's "Dialogue Partner System"), have been important for forging links between countries in the region, as has the more recent ASEAN Forum, a security-oriented series of meetings. ASEAN is dealt with in more detail in the following chapter.

The grouping that has perhaps enjoyed most publicity recently is APEC,, established in 1989 (Low 1991) as a result of an Australian initiative, but which has only recently taken on a more structured form.[7] According to the original idea, APEC was modeled on the Organization of Economic Cooperation and Development (Harris 1994). The end result was a less formalized, consultative organization, though. Even APEC, which is a governmental body, albeit a highly nonformal one, has taken a careful, step-by-step view of its decision-making process, an attitude no doubt necessary in order to accommodate the diversity of the participating countries. In this respect, APEC has functioned much in the same way as ASEAN.[8]

Officially, the aim of APEC is to serve as a discussion forum for issues related to trade and economic cooperation, to enhance cooperation between developed and developing countries, work against barriers to trade of goods, services, and technology, and to work as a lobby group to resist protectionism in international trade. The aim is explicitly on "open regionalism," not at forming an exclusive trade bloc (cf. Elek 1995). The activity of APEC evolves around annual meetings of foreign and economic ministers, but the organization has several committees and working groups at a lower level as well. PECC has an official status as observer, while the contacts to PBEC and PAFTAD are unofficial but apparently quite close (Union of International Organizations 1995: 88–89). As a matter of fact, APEC has based its agenda to a great extent on, especially, PECC but also PAFTAD and PBEC (Harris 1994). PECC has been seen, after the instigation of APEC, as "the research and support arm of APEC" (Higgott 1993), providing analytical back-up for the grouping.

Originally, APEC was formed—at least partly—because of concern about increasingly inward-looking economic integration in Europe and North America.

Recently the organization to an increasing degree has taken on the task of actively liberalizing trade in the whole Asia-Pacific region. The higher profile has been underlined by the fact that summits have been held annually during the last few years. The recent pledge, at the Bogor Summit in 1994, to create an area for free trade and investment by the year 2020 (for industrialized economies, 2010) (*ASEAN Economic Bulletin* 1995), was reiterated and concretized at the Osaka Summit in 1995. From January 1997 a detailed "action agenda" is supposed to set the pace for implementing the commitment (Bergsten 1996). As pointed out by Elek (1995), however, the scope for cooperation within APEC stretches far from mere elimination of tariffs. Other impediments to trade are equally important, such as unilateral threats, infrastructural shortages, and different standards and procedures.

The organizational rigor of APEC has been strengthened as well with the establishment of a permanent secretariat in Singapore in 1992, although its administrative bureaucracy is still quite small and powerless. It appears that the very cautious approach taken by most APEC members early on has now given way to a higher degree of commitment. It has to be remembered, though, that very little in the way of concrete achievements have been reached so far despite official optimism. Commitments actually made are usually at a very general level and aim at points far in the future for which present leaders do not carry any responsibility. As recently pointed out (Forbes 1996), there is no real obligation, apart from peer pressure, to honor deadlines and targets of APEC, and hence the member countries are free to set their own agendas. Considering the heterogeneous membership of APEC, this may be regarded as an advantage, too, at least as long as real progress is being made.

APEC is a large organization. For instance, its members account for 40 percent of total world trade and half of world output. Among its members are the world's three largest economies: the United States, Japan, and China. While this is a strength in itself, and is likely to help avoid a development toward an exclusive trade bloc (cf. Bergsten 1996; *The Economist,* November 11, 1995), it is also a weakness inasmuch as its members are disparate and may have quite differing views on the role of the organization. In particular, the legalistic approach of the United States versus a "flexible," consensus mode of functioning, more natural in Asia, seem to have caused friction. The former view is more in accordance with a formalization of APEC, held together by binding international agreements. According to the latter point of view, APEC is not primarily about trade but about promoting Asian harmony (*Economist,* November 11, 1995).[9] The related question of whether liberalization within the organization should automatically be extended to nonmember countries as well is open, too. In  several cases there are, or have been, serious trade disputes between members. That APEC has so far made commitments only concerning a distant future is somewhat discouraging, even if these commitments in themselves are far-reaching. The above-mentioned "action agenda" has also been criticized for being too vague to be effective (*Economist,* November 25, 1995).

As noted by Harris (1991), in spite of all the organizations mentioned, their number and extension are still quite insignificant if the region is compared with Europe and North America. A consequence of this has evidently been a certain lack of information and communication between people involved in international relations, which has rendered intraregional interaction less significant than it could have been. What is happening now may be a kind of catch-up process in this respect. The organizations commented on above are all strongly interrelated in the sense that their membership is overlapping. All of them have strong connections to their domestic political and economic elites. Hence it is likely that the organizations have developed considerable synergy effects, even if these are not readily visible.

## THE "LEADERSHIP" ISSUE

Discussions of formal economic cooperation in the Asia-Pacific (or East Asian) region have inevitably also focused on the question of "leadership." In particular, the apparent reluctance of Japan to take on more responsibility as the biggest and most developed country in the region has been the object for much debate (see, e.g., Rix 1993). Japan's presence is strong in East Asia, however, and its influence greater than it may appear on the surface. By and large, Japan has been reluctant to function as a regional spokesman, however. Despite this, it is hard to envisage an alternative leader. China, for instance, is still too undeveloped and chaotic to be able to take up this mantle. The fact that the country is still communist, even if this is increasingly a facade, is also a problem in this context. There are signs that ASEAN has now assumed an unofficial collective leadership, through its postministerial conferences with "dialogue partners," the ASEAN Regional Forum in the political realm and others. The heterogeneity of ASEAN itself is likely to be an obstacle for assuming a very assertive role, however. The gradual enlarging of ASEAN is likely to make the organization weaker, not stronger, at least in the short run. Recently APEC has been proposed as a leader (Higgott 1993). Today, however, this organization is too weak to assume such leadership.

All in all, with the possible exception of ASEAN, these Asia-Pacific economic groupings are quite loose; they are neither organizations proper or trading blocs but rather discussion clubs for enhancing the interests of the participating countries and cooperation between them (cf. Hughes 1991; Langhammer 1991a). In spite of those attempts, considerable trade and investment barriers remain. The perceived results may depend on what one looks for, however. It is fair to recognize that the fact that most Asian-Pacific organizations and groupings have a very light organization and a low degree of formalization may not necessarily imply that their de facto achievements have been negligible. Since the results cannot usually be related to formal decisions within those organizations, however, their role is very hard to nail down in a measurable way. It has to be recognized that much of the efforts have not aimed at creating exclusive trading blocs, as a presumed counterweight to the European Community and the emerging North American free trade area, as demonstrated very clearly in speeches by, for example, former prime ministers Bob Hawke of Australia and Lee Kuan Yew of Singapore (Hughes 1991). Rather the promotion of a liberal, multilateral trade regime has been stressed. It has also been argued (Harris 1994) that the recent progress made in cooperation between governments would not have been possible without the long dialogues that had taken place earlier within the nongovernmental organizations.

## GROWTH TRIANGLES

A new type of organized developmental zones has begun to develop in several East Asian countries, the so-called growth triangles. These are often rather informally conceived subregions consisting of parts of two or several countries, where the different parties cooperate in order to take advantages of complementarities between the countries. These arrangements are usually recognized by respective governments, but the private sector is the driving force. The oldest and best known of these growth triangles is the one that encompasses Singapore, the Malaysian state of Johor, and the Riau archipelago in Indonesia. Singapore, in particular, has been able to take advantage of the scheme by relocating industries that are losing their competitiveness due to rising costs in Singapore. The link between Johor and Riau has remained weak, however. In ASEAN, two more "triangles" are emerging: the Northern Triangle, involving parts of Indonesia, Malaysia, and Thailand (with Penang Island in Malaysia as its center), and the East ASEAN Growth Area, comprising Brunei, Mindanao in the Philippines, Sabah and Sarawak in Malaysia, and Kalimantan and Sulawesi in Indonesia. All these are considerably less developed than the Singapore–Johor–Riau triangle. A similar, although still much more informal, "triangle" is farther north, encompassing Taiwan, Hong Kong, and the southern provinces of China, particularly Guangdong and Fujien. Discussions have also taken place about this kind of arrangement in the Tumen River area in Russia, involving Korea (North and South) and China.

## CONCLUSIONS

The Asia-Pacific region still has comparatively few and weak formal economic organizations. This is due partly to historical reasons but also to the fact that the region is very large and the countries that are part of it are extremely disparate in almost every sense of the word. The growing economic significance of the region, paired with increasing interdependence and thus both greater potential gains to be made and greater potential risks for friction to emerge, has put pressure on the decision makers to build institutions able to handle the situation.

While cooperation in the broad sense usually concerns international public goods and externalities, with all the problems related to this type of goods, integration is more specific and implies unification of national markets and, at the extreme end, a common economic policy. In the case of cooperation, most activity has been developed by ASEAN, but due to the wide range of undertakings that are possible under this rubric, a general assessment is very difficult to make. (Much cooperation also falls under the category of "silent diplomacy.")

No significant integration scheme is still firmly in place in East Asia, although limited attempts have been made under the auspices of ASEAN, which is discussed in Chapter 7. Two important plans for integration are now under way, however, aiming at virtually free trade in ASEAN and among the APEC members by the early twenty-first century. Both plans are fairly recent, and it is too early to say what the final result will be.

## NOTES

1. Integration may also mean only that two or several countries are involved in extensive exchange of goods, capital and so on, without formal agreements.

2. The two latter are particularly important objects for cooperation because they are frequently used as nontariff trade barriers.

3. To be exact, there are some differences between the effects of customs unions and free trade areas. The fact that a free trade area does not have a uniform tariff barrier causes some differences compared to customs unions. The welfare effects generally appear more favorable in the case of a free trade area, although the significance of this result should not be exaggerated (cf. Robson 1984: 23–30).

4. The members are from: Canada, Chile, Colombia, Mexico, Peru, United States, Brunei, China, Hong Kong, Indonesia, Japan, South Korea, Malaysia, Philippines, Singapore, Taiwan, Thailand, Australia, New Zealand, and Russia.

5. The members are from: Canada, Chile, Colombia, Mexico, Peru, United States, China, Hong Kong, Japan, South Korea, Malaysia, Philippines, Taiwan, Australia, Fiji, New Zealand, and Russia.

6. The idea was mooted by Professor Kiyoshi Kojima (Woods 1991).

7. Members of the organization are: Canada, Chile, Mexico, the United States, Brunei, China, Hong Kong, Indonesia, Japan, South Korea, Malaysia, the Philippines, Singapore, Taiwan, Thailand, Australia, New Zealand, and Papua New Guinea.

8. According to the "Kuching Consensus," adopted by ASEAN in 1990, a consensus type of decision making is a precondition for ASEAN's participation in APEC (Elek 1995).

9. In this context it is worthwhile to remember that APEC has important security connotations, too, although it is not conceived as a security forum but an economic grouping.

# 7

## ASEAN—A Success Story?

### INTRODUCTION

This chapter examines one of the oldest surviving economic organizations in East Asia, the Association of Southeast Asian Nations, with the aim of evaluating what purposes it has fulfilled, to what extent it has been beneficial for its member countries, and whether it can be considered a useful model of cooperation for other countries in the region and outside it. ASEAN comprises some of the most dynamic economies in the world. Hence one would be inclined a priori to draw the conclusion that ASEAN, as a cooperative organization, has been successful. A closer look indicates, however, that such a conclusion may be premature, although the result of an evaluation depends, to a considerable extent, on what criteria for success one chooses to apply.

### ECONOMIC COOPERATION THE ASEAN WAY

ASEAN was founded in 1967 by Indonesia, Malaysia, the Philippines, Singapore, and Thailand after several abortive attempts to set up organizations for cooperation in Southeast Asia. Brunei joined ASEAN in 1984 and Vietnam in 1995. The organization has survived to this day, being now a major force affecting economic and political developments in East Asia and the Asia-Pacific region. This is the case despite the fact that the original prospects for successful cooperation between the member countries were not particularly favorable, due to historical and political differences and to the fact that the countries to a great extent were oriented toward third countries in their external economic relations.

At the outset, ASEAN was established primarily with regional security and political stability in mind, even if the so-called Bangkok declaration, which marks the foundation of the organization, emphasizes economic progress and social and cultural development and not political cooperation (cf., e.g., Rieger 1989; Rolls 1991). This is certainly not surprising, considering the many problems in regional relations at the time. The Vietnam war was going on, the situation in Indonesia was volatile before General Suharto's coup, there were the Indonesian "konfrontasi" (confrontation) against Malaysia, unsettled territorial claims, and other conflicts.

The proposal to form the organization was seen as a unique opportunity to secure lasting peace in the region. It has also been argued that Indonesia, which was in great need of development assistance from the West, could make use of the organization in order to boost its credibility, and in return was willing to cooperate with its smaller neighbors. This constellation, however, secured an implicit leading role for Indonesia, the least developed member, in the association, which partly explains the slow pace of progress of different cooperation schemes (cf. Gill 1987: 14, 111).

The Vietnamese invasion of Cambodia in 1978 contributed strongly to fostering a feeling of unity between the members of the association (cf., for instance, Colbert 1986: 200). It seems quite clear that the organization indeed has been of great value in promoting peace and stability in the region. In fact, it has been maintained that ASEAN is, above all, a "political process" (Rolls 1991).

The economic benefits of the favorable political development can hardly be overestimated (cf. Ariff and Tan, J.L.H. 1992), even if the exact results are well-nigh impossible to measure. The first few years of the life of ASEAN were important also in the sense that they prepared the foundation for more intimate cooperation. Without the perceived external threat from, above all, advancing communism in the region, the organization may not have survived in the long run, however. Historically and geographically, Southeast Asia is not a natural entity but a highly heterogeneous group of political units with very different backgrounds, a fact that no doubt caused difficulties for the cooperation within ASEAN to get started. A particular problem seems to have been the perceived risk for a polarization effect (explained above in Chapter 6), particularly as the most developed members happen to be the smallest ones, a fact that may aggravate any scheme for redistribution of the gains (Wong 1989). (On the other hand, smallness should guarantee that these countries cannot absorb unlimited amounts of gains either.)

ASEAN still has a very light administrative apparatus of its own, consisting of a secretariat in Jakarta, organized only in the early 1980s (Rieger 1991: 17). This is an administrative and coordinating body only, with no independent decision-making authority of its own. The decision-making process used in ASEAN can best be characterized by the term consensus (cf. Wong 1985), where the decisions are made by committees and working groups at different administrative levels (Thambipillai and Saravanamuttu 1985: 23). While this has probably been a precondition for the organization to survive—and in any case the result of a deliberate choice of the members—and despite the advantages of such a model (the outcome of a consensus decision is that of a "positive sum" rather than a zero-sum, win-lose game that is the likely result of many voting decisions), it has also been an excuse for hiding disagreements between the partners (see Thambipillai and Saravanamuttu 1985: 13). The bureaucrats have also tended to proceed very cautiously and have been carefully safeguarding "national interests." Moreover, the progress achieved has, as indicated above, effectively been limited by the "slowest" member, usually Indonesia (cf. Ariff 1992). The consensus principle was recently modified at the Singapore Summit in 1992. While it is still important for ASEAN to show consensus in external dealings, it is now possible to go ahead with a cooperation scheme if two or more members can agree (Okamoto 1995).

It is an acknowledged fact that the achievements of ASEAN have not always been impressive. The less than satisfactory results in, above all, economic cooperation may indeed, to some extent, be related to an inadequate "machinery" of the association. On the other hand, an advantage of this decentralized structure, except inexpensiveness, has no doubt been the advancement of a broad engagement in the activities of ASEAN at the national level (Chng 1990). Having said that, one must bear in mind that an extensive bureaucracy with some independent decision-making power of its own would apparently have been impossible to create due to political reasons. The member states have been fiercely independent-minded and have consistently emphasized their sovereignty and any kind of supranational decision-making has been out of the question (see, e.g., the formulations in the ASEAN Concord of 1986 (Rieger 1991: 106)). However, it seems evident that more technical and professional support for committee work and so on would improve the efficiency of the organization, reducing the number of meetings and the amount of international traveling necessary to keep the association going (cf. Akrasanee 1984: 41–42; see also Lee 1991). As for the future, its seems likely that such an administrative machinery—primarily in the form of a strengthened secretariat—has to be put in place, particularly as the number of decisions to be made increases along with the deepening of cooperation. Some steps in that direction have recently been taken.

The specific economic objectives of ASEAN were vague and unstructured in the beginning. It took nearly ten years after the foundation of ASEAN until its economic character began to emerge. (Also, in other respects, the concrete results accomplished during the first ten-year period are hard to pinpoint.) ASEAN is neither a customs union nor (yet) a free trade area, although a discussion on forming a limited free trade area and a payments union took place as early as 1971 at the Manila Summit (Suriyamongkol 1988: 68; Gill 1987: 99). At that time, however, the larger member countries were not prepared to expose their nascent industrial sectors to any degree of "unnecessary" foreign competition.

Until recently, the term *integration* has been consistently avoided in the context of ASEAN by the members of the organization, and the vaguer but more comprehensive term *cooperation* has been preferred (Wong 1985). The agenda of the organization consists of a number of cooperation programs. It is characteristic of the cautious proceeding of the early ASEAN that the content of its economic cooperation to begin with was largely the result of external advice. Many of the cooperation programs originated in the so-called Robinson (or Kansu) Report, the published results and recommendations of a UN-initiated investigation (United Nations 1974). The spirit of the report was very much that of (regional) import substitution and the primary recommendations were limited intraregional trade liberalization combined with a coordinated industrialization policy (Arndt and Garnaut 1979; Rieger 1989; Langhammer 1991a). Many of the specific cooperation programs embarked upon later emanate from the recommendations of the Robinson Report. The report has, however, with the benefit of hindsight, been sharply criticized for leading the cooperation into unfruitful projects and creating bureaucracy and regional monopolies as well as fostering a generally inward-looking attitude (Yam et al. 1992; see also Gill 1987: 38).

Hence an important reason for the limited success of the major economic cooperation programs of the association may have been excessive reliance on state planning, especially as the bureaucratic infrastructure necessary for such a strategy was weak and divided, the common secretariat being little more than a "mailbox." To this may be added a certain degree of indecisiveness and a lack of specific goals for the process. In other cases, such as the trade liberalization program, the relative failure may rather have been due to the timing factor. Manufacturing was simply too protected in the large member countries, and a long process of liberalization has been necessary to prepare the industry for foreign competition. Another factor is no doubt the multinational companies, far more important for the host countries today than ten to fifteen years ago. These companies are as a rule very competitive and tend to argue for trade liberalization. With the benefit of hindsight , and using the experiences from similar attempts in other parts of the world, there are good reasons to assume that an attempt at integration proper in the 1970s and early 1980s would not have been a success. Today the situation has changed to a considerable extent.

In the economic realm, ASEAN, until recently, has been active primarily within five different programs: (1) the ASEAN Industrial Projects (AIP), (2) the ASEAN Industrial Complementation (AIC); (3) the ASEAN Industrial Joint Ventures (AIJV); (4) the Preferential Trading Arrangement (PTA); and (5) the ASEAN Dialogue Partner System (ADPS).

Of these instruments of cooperation, only the PTA is directly a device for integration, while the first two programs were rather instruments for planned regional industrialization. AIJV, finally, can be characterized as a regional incentive scheme, while ADPS is a device for handling external economic relations with ASEAN's chief trade partners.

The AIPs (from 1976; the first project was inaugurated in 1984; Rieger 1991: 18) aimed at providing the governments with an instrument to assign new, government-initiated, large-scale industrial projects to different member countries. The leading idea was that, in general, only one plant of a kind should be built in the region and that this plant should serve all member countries. The rationale for this was, of course, to permit maximum utilization of potential scale economies as well as comparative advantages within the organization (cf. Arndt and Garnaut 1979).

The actual results of this program remained rather insignificant. Only two projects were completed out of five planned (one for each member nation), one of which would probably have been taken on in any case. The problem was that the governments were not willing to relinquish their freedom to invest in whatever they please. As a matter of fact, even the two projects actually realized were very much pursued as national endeavors (cf. Suriyamongkol 1988: 188). The five original projects have also been criticized for having been quickly outlined and badly planned. The perceived need to accomplish visible results quickly led to improvisation and insufficient consideration, in the form of, for instance, feasibility studies, of the problems involved. As noted by Akrasanee (1984: 35), one obvious reason for this is the lack of an institution capable of identifying suitable AIPs. The private sector avoided getting involved in these projects (cf., e.g., Suriyamongkol 1988: 117, 121 and Wong 1989).

All in all, the projects were rather ill prepared and did not have the real regional backing they were supposed to have had (Suriyamongkol 1988: 139). According to Langhammer (1991a), the fundamental reason for the problem is that a program of this type is really characteristic of a planned economy. The ASEAN countries are not planned economies, however, with the allocation monopoly that would have implied. The national industrial sectors jealously strove to keep foreign potential suppliers away. It is difficult to come up with well-based arguments in favor of supranational government-led industrial location anyway. The market system should be able to do that, or, in the case of very undeveloped capital markets, the single governments may step in. This conclusion is corroborated by several experiences from similar projects in other parts of the world (cf., e.g., Reynolds 1992).

The same type of argument can largely be used also in the case of the AIC program (in operation since 1981). The aim here was toward intraindustry (horizontal) specialization in the private sector, where the production of different components of a final product was to be located in different countries. The results have also been poor in this case. Only one project, concerning automotive components, within the so-called Brand to Brand Complementation (BBC) agreement (see, e.g., Steven 1996: 141), has been implemented, with rather negligible (US$ 1 million) effect on intra-ASEAN trade. Wong (1989) estimates that the cost incurred by realizing this project is likely to have exceeded the benefits.

One important reason for the lackluster performance of the AIC program has no doubt been bureaucracy. In this program it was the task of the ASEAN Chamber of Commerce to identify and promote suitable cooperation objects, as well as to work as an intermediary between the governments and the private enterprises. At least four of the (originally) five member states were to participate in each project (Wong 1985). The basic problem, however, seems to be that there is no reason why the markets could not take care of the issue, except for existing trade impediments. Government intervention was used here as a substitute for eliminating those trade barriers.

The AIJV program was conceived somewhat later than the two already dealt with (in 1983), partly in order to avoid some of the problems inherent in the other programs. Also in this case, specific manipulation with trade barriers has been made use of in order to make cooperation otherwise not deemed profitable more attractive. (The AIJV products qualify for tariff preferences in all ASEAN countries, after a transition period of four years; Rieger 1989.) The idea was partly to avoid the broad engagement of countries required in the AIC—two ASEAN partners would be enough—and to facilitate cooperation in smaller ventures. The bureaucracy involved is much less elaborate, too (Wong 1985). Quite a few projects of this category have been approved, although the program has hardly been a stunning success. The bureaucracy involved in the approval process has been a major drawback, though, particularly at an earlier stage. At the Manila Summit in 1987 the system was changed and simplified. In the new system there are lists of products approved in advance (Ariff 1988: 162). Thus the projects do not have to be approved one by one. On the whole, however, ASEAN firms seem to prefer joint ventures with partners from outside the region (Naya and Plummer 1991). Also intra-ASEAN joint venture projects are more often outside the AIJV system than within. Bureaucracy and loss of time often outweigh the potential utility of an AIJV project. In fact, the AIJV program is of course also a free trade substitute. Trade liberalization would render organized cooperation programs of this type redundant.

The Preferential Trade Arrangement (initiated in Manila 1977) used to be the integration instrument proper in the economic-political arsenal of ASEAN. As pointed out by Langhammer (1991a), it was also crucial for the feasibility of the other types of cooperation. By and large, this scheme also seems to have resulted in mixed success at most, apparently because of a small coverage and too small tariff cuts. In fact, potentially tradable products regularly tended to end up on the exemption list of "sensitive" items, that is, the infant industry argument was invoked. Moreover, the demand on local content is high for a product to qualify (50 percent after 1984) (Wong 1989). The scheme has not had any fixed goal to strive toward either (cf. Akrasanee 1984: 36). Although the Manila Summit in 1987 "in principle" adopted a five-year timetable to include 50 percent of intra-ASEAN trade under the PTA scheme (Frost 1990: 25), the results were not impressive. Nontariff barriers more important than the tariffs also seem to have a part in the poor result (cf., e.g., Rahman and Mansor 1987). According to Rieger (1989), not more than 0.4 percent of the total intraregional trade had been created by the PTA system (cf. also Devan 1987) by the late 1980s.

As is the custom in ASEAN, the dialogue partner system (ADPS) does not delegate decision power to supranational organs, but requires the governments of the ASEAN countries to find areas of mutual interest to raise in the discussions with the trade partners. The utility provided by the Dialogue Partner System (originated at the Kuala Lumpur Summit in 1977 (Curry 1991; Rieger 1991: 16)) is a forum for discussions between the ASEAN member countries and its major trade partners, the United States, Canada, the EC, Japan, Australia, New Zealand, and, later, South Korea. China and India were approved as dialogue partners at the Singapore Summit in early 1992 (*Far Eastern Economic Review*, February 6, 1992). The United Nations' Development Program (UNDP) is also a dialogue partner. Originally, an agreement similar to that of the Lomé convention between the European Communities (now transformed into the European Union) and former colonies of the European countries seems to have been aimed at (cf. Suriyamongkol 1988: 169), but the subsequent development has been more ad hoc.

On the part of ASEAN, the work on the Dialogue Partner System is organized by assigning each member country one major trade partner. It is the responsibility of this member to coordinate the views of the other members (cf. Thambipillai and Saravanamuttu 1985: 19). Much of the work is nowadays concentrated in the so-called post-ministerial conferences (PMC), which are held after the annual meeting of the ASEAN foreign ministers, beginning in Manila 1981 (cf., e.g., Hoon 1990: 20). The substance of the negotiations has been primarily questions concerning market access (Ariff and Tan, J.L.H. 1992). At the recent Singapore Summit the scope of the ADPS was enlarged to encompassing political and security-related issues as well (*Straits Times*, January 30, 1992; see also July 24, 1991).

The common external trade policy, according to Langhammer (1991a), is a true supranational public good which cannot be provided individually by each country on its own. The dialogue is important particularly due to the indisputable fact that ASEAN has profited from relatively free international trade, and that the present threat of a more protectionist international trade climate would be extremely unwelcome for the members of this organization (cf., e.g., Albrecht 1990: 115).

The success of the ADPS has been perceived differently by different authors, which is hardly surprising considering the immaterial nature of the "product" the system is supposed to deliver. For instance, Langhammer (1991a) has a very positive view, like Wong (1989), while Chng (1990) deems the results "disappointing." The results seem to have been fairly good as far as soliciting aid and technical assistance is concerned, but less so for the original main goal of the process, improving market access to the dialogue partners (Akrasanee 1984: 31–32 and 36–37). Everybody seems to agree, however, that the system has been conducive to raising the profile and status of ASEAN in an international context.

## PROSPECTS FOR FURTHER INTEGRATION

The rather modest achievements of ASEAN in the economic field have been increasingly recognized by the member states and researchers alike. At the same time, the global economic environment is changing rapidly. Particularly the tendency toward forming trade blocs in Europe and the Americas and, until recently, the sluggish progress of the so-called Uruguay Round (the trade liberalization talks within GATT) pose a new challenge for the association. With the declaration of the intention to form the ASEAN Free Trade Area, the so-called Singapore Declaration, originally proposed in 1991 by the then prime minister of Thailand, Anand Panyarachun, the trade preference system of ASEAN goes into a new era. The interesting question in this context is, of course, whether AFTA is likely to be a good idea from the regional development point of view, considering the less than encouraging experiences from other parts of the world (for some examples, see Blomqvist et al. 1992).

The degree of economic integration in ASEAN has been, and still is, rather low, both formally and de facto. The importance of intra-ASEAN trade is not great—especially if Singapore is excluded—and no clear time trend can be discerned (see International Monetary Fund, various years). An obvious reason for the small trade volumes is the similar structure of the larger ASEAN economies, Brunei and Singapore being special cases. Another reason is probably also that a significant part of the manufacturing industry in the region is foreign-owned, and thus often vertically integrated with the home country's industry. (In spite of that, the multinational companies are likely to welcome a free trade area, due to the obvious rationalization possibilities within ASEAN which that would offer.) The high degree of intraindustry trade between ASEAN and Japan and the NICs, respectively, discussed in Chapter 3, seems to be an indication of that. Intraindustry trade within ASEAN is, as a matter of fact, largely bilateral trade between Singapore and each of the other countries (Imada et al. 1992: 13). Hence the picture of intra-ASEAN trade changes considerably when Singapore is included. This demonstrates very clearly the pivotal role of Singapore in the region. The reason for this is hardly ASEAN as such, however, but the traditional role of Singapore as an entrepôt for the region.

As for the trade patterns, it should also be noted that there have been strong structural changes in the exports of the ASEAN countries during the last couple of decades. Between 1970 and 1989 the export share of manufactured products increased from 11 to 58.3 percent. For the exports to the United States this share was as high as 79.8 percent, and for the exports to the NIEs (Singapore excluded), 58.4 percent. Also in the intra-ASEAN trade, manufactured products predominate, with 62.5 percent of the exports. For the exports to Japan, however, raw materials are still the most important product category (Ariff and Tan, E.C. 1992).

The intra-ASEAN trade is predominantly intraindustry trade, if a three-digit SITC classification is applied (Ariff and Tan, E.C. 1992). ASEAN as an organization probably has been conducive to this, but to what extent is hard to specify. The high shares of manufactures in the trade with third countries (but also to some extent as for intra-ASEAN trade) are primarily a consequence of the foreign investment in the region. These investments have contributed not only capital and technology, but also market access and marketing know-how (cf. Ariff and Tan, E.C. 1992; Blomström 1990: 7).

De facto economic integration has also recently been proliferating through informal economic areas transcending national borders, where differing comparative advantages can be taken advantage of. These are the so-called growth triangles, briefly mentioned in Chapter 6, the best known and most developed of which is the Singapore–Johor–Riau triangle, which encompasses parts of three different countries: Indonesia, Malaysia, and Singapore. In ASEAN there are two other such areas as well, even if they are still in their infancy, that is, the "Northern Triangle" comprising the state of Penang in Malaysia, southern Thailand, and the northern part of Sumatra in Indonesia, and the "East ASEAN Growth Area" engaging southern parts of the Philippines, the Malaysian states of Sabah and Sarawak, Brunei, and Kalimantan and Sulawesi in Indonesia (Kumar 1993; Kumar and Siddique 1994; and Chia and Lee 1993). The rationale of growth triangles is the possibilities they offer for exploiting complementary endowments of factors of production. These projects are characterized by a limited engagement of governments which have largely confined themselves to providing infrastructure. Instead, the private sectors are the driving force as they indeed are behind much of the actual regional integration achieved (cf. ESCAP 1994: 52). These arrangements may well be of interest for overseas investors as well, as the use of resources from different countries is facilitated.

## THE AFTA ISSUE

The possibility of developing a free trade area with some amount of success would to a considerable extent be dependent on whether the intraregional trade is extensive and on the increase within the present system, indicating increasing interdependence and intraindustry complementarity between the countries. As we have seen, such signs are not too strong. Hence the potential trade diversion effect (imports from an efficient external producer are replaced by imports from a less efficient member country) may be considerable. To avoid serious distortions it would be important to keep the trade barriers toward third countries at a reasonable level. In fact, what is done about third country access to the markets of the free trade area may very well dominate the rest of the effects, especially in very open economies such as the ASEAN countries. (The general attitude in ASEAN to date has been one of increasing openness, however.) There is likely to be some trade creation as well (inefficent domestic production is replaced by goods produced more efficiently in another member country), due to the rather significant trade barriers between the member countries that still exist in many cases.

It is impossible to assess exactly the effects of a free trade area in ASEAN. According to Imada et al. (1992), the effects on production and trade are likely to be positive, although rather small. Others such as Panagariya (1994) have been more pessimistic, concluding that the net effect may be negative. This is because any effects from preferential trade must emanate from those member countries that are most protected. The same countries will have to bear the negative effect of possible trade diversion, however. A very large part of the intra-ASEAN trade is in fact bilateral trade between Singapore and the other members. As Singapore (as Brunei and largely also Malaysia), have liberal trade regimes already there will be no immediate benefits for the trade partners (cf. *Economist*, September 16, 1995). This may help to explain the greater willingness in ASEAN to implement unilateral, nondiscriminatory liberalization rather than forming inward-looking blocs.

Despite this rather subdued judgment on the effects of AFTA, it is likely that its dynamic effects would be more substantial. In particular, the effects on FDI should be positive as a larger "home market" should be more attractive to investors than the present, rather divided local market. The effects through increasing competition on local firms should be wholesome as well, and facilitate both inter- and intraindustrial specialization. At the same time, drawing on earlier experience, there is reason to believe that the formation of AFTA will be accompanied by further dismantling of the trade barriers of the member countries against third countries.

The major question mark as far as AFTA is concerned is its cautious timetable. Originally the establishment of the area was scheduled to take place in fifteen years. Also the complicated vehicle for tariff reductions approved by the member states—the Common Effective Preferential Tariff (CEPT) scheme—has raised doubts about the commitment of all member countries to live up to the Singapore Declaration. After a rather sluggish start, at least partly due to the complex nature of CEPT, and practical problems with the tariff nomenclature, the implementation of tariff reductions is now well under way (ASEAN 1995, East Asia Analytical Unit 1994). Moreover, all specific tariffs and so on have to be converted into *ad valorem* tax rates (*ASEAN Economic InfoView* 1994). The CEPT Agreement also contains other elements, such as harmonization of standards, reciprocal recognition of tests and certification of products, rules for competition and FDI, and macroeconomic consultation (Chng 1995).

In addition to tariffs, nontariff barriers may be a problem, too (cf. Kumar 1991), when the free trade area is set up. Serious efforts are presently being made to dismantle such impediments according to a schedule envisaged by ASEAN officials (Chng 1995: 5; Wong 1995). Additionally, an ASEAN Framework Agreement in Services was signed in December 1995 (*ASEAN Economic Bulletin* 1996a). This agreement will be made as a complement to the recent General Agreement on Trade in Services (GATS). The agreement aims at eliminating "substantially" all existing discriminatory measures and market access limitations among the member countries "within a reasonable time frame" (article 3). Four areas have been specifically targeted (although not mentioned in the agreement itself): financial services, tourism, infrastructure development, and transport and communications (*Asian Business Review,* October 1995; *ASEAN Economic Bulletin* 1996a). Rules on intellectual property have also been looked into, and a framework agreement was also signed in December 1995 (*ASEAN Economic Bulletin* 1996b). Among other things, the agreement concerns the intention to set up ASEAN-wide patent and trademark systems. As far as the specific contents of the two agreements are concerned, they are formulated in very general terms, according to the traditional custom of ASEAN, and leave the real degree of commitment to be determined by the national governments.

According to the original AFTA agreement, members were allowed three years before starting to dismantle their trade barriers as of January 1, 1993. Ultimately a tariff level of 5 percent or less is the goal of the scheme. Products with a minimum of 40 percent ASEAN contents are eligible for trade liberalization within AFTA. An exclusion list on specific products at the HS (Harmonized System) 8–9 digit level was allowed, but the members committed themselves to abolishing all remaining barriers also for these products at the end of the eighth year. A "fast track" program was also initiated, covering fifteen product groups and comprising nearly 40 percent of ASEAN trade. The "fast track" comprises the following product groups: fats and oils, mineral products, chemicals, plastics, hides and leather, pulp and paper, textiles and apparel, cement, gems, base metals and metal articles, machinery and electrical appliances, and miscellaneous manufactured articles (ASEAN 1995: 17). In this group, tariffs should be reduced to less then 5 percent within seven to ten years. According to figures from early 1994, CEPT covered, depending on country, between 56 and 100 percent of the export value of the organization and between 76 and 100 percent of the import value (ASEAN 1995: 42). Vietnam, on becoming a member in July 1995, agreed to join CEPT on January 1, 1996 and complete the country's implementation of the agreement by 2006 (*ASEAN Update,* July 1995).

Recently (at the economic ministers' meeting in Chiang Mai in September 1994) the time frame for implementing AFTA was revised in order to achieve faster results. By the year 2000, all products in the "fast track" must have CEPT tariff rates at 5 percent or less. According to the "normal track," tariffs will be lowered to not more than 20 percent by 1998 and to 5 percent by 2003.

The new virtually free trade regime, including also all agricultural products, now is to be established by January 1, 2003, five years earlier than originally planned. At the same time, a decision was taken to abolish the temporary exclusion list gradually, allowing members to exclude "sensitive" products from the scheme *(Asiaweek,* October 5, 1994; *ASEAN Economic Bulletin* 1994). A recent initiative by the Sultan of Brunei, Hassanal Bolkiah, backed by Singapore's Trade and Industry minister, Yeo Cheow Tong, calls for a still faster rate of implementation with the deadline brought forward to the year 2000 (Wong 1995). It is still too early to assess the real progress on this front, however, even if it is already evident that many officials would prefer not to take the risk to force the time schedule too much. What seems clear, despite this, is that the commitment to AFTA is stronger than what was the case for the earlier cooperation schemes (Chng 1995: 4).

In Table 7.1 the number of products (tariff lines) in CEPT are presented; 88 percent of the tariff lines in ASEAN are presently included in the CEPT scheme, each line with a schedule for tariff reductions (ASEAN 1995).

**Table 7.1**
**Number of Items under Different Treatment (tariff lines in CEPT)**

| Country | Fast Track | Normal Track | Temporary Exclusion |
|---|---|---|---|
| Brunei | 2,377 | 3,618 | 236 |
| Indonesia | 2,819 | 4,539 | 1,648 |
| Malaysia | 2,985 | 5,710 | 621 |
| Philippines | 960 | 3,432 | 694 |
| Singapore | 2,183 | 3,473 | 1 |
| Vietnam | .. | .. | .. |
| Total | 14,855 | 25,918 | 3,322 |

*Note:* .. = not available
*Source:* ASEAN 1995: 15.

## THE CHALLENGE OF THE FUTURE

Several recent developments have posed a challenge to the future viability of ASEAN. While this may not render the region less interesting from a business point of view, it may reduce its attractiveness as a host for FDI, given that the alternative is further integration. In the political realm, the end of the cold war apparently eliminated one of the central reasons for upholding the organization and, for that matter, for its coherence. This does not mean, however, that the security problems in the region are solved, and it is likely that ASEAN will continue to play a role in that context, regardless of economic progress.

ASEAN is now poised to realize one of its long-term objectives: to incorporate all ten countries of Southeast Asia in the organization. This process may well be finished by the end of the century despite the fact that the present nonmembers are not easy to admit due to both economic and political reasons. One of the major difficulties inherent in increasing the number of members is also ASEAN's consensus model of decision making which by necessity becomes more and more complicated the larger the number of participants is. As mentioned in the theoretical discussion in Chapter 6, there is some evidence that the marginal cost of enlarging international organizations tends to rise steeply, while the marginal benefit for the earlier members is likely to be falling. At any rate, a larger organization would necessitate an overhaul of the mechanisms of decision making, but ASEAN is evidently not ready for major changes yet.

A second problem is the role of ASEAN in the context of other, existing or proposed, economic organizations in the Asia-Pacific region, such as APEC, PECC, and EAEC. The recent strengthening of the organizational framework of ASEAN, for example, the appointment of a secretary-general with ministerial status, and the decision to hold summits at a regular three-year interval (Antolik 1992), are measures that are likely to have been necessary, if not sufficient, for securing a future for the Association.

As far as ASEAN's economic justification is concerned, the recent launching of the World Trade Organization (WTO) and the pledge by the Asia-Pacific Economic Cooperation forum to create an area for free trade and investment by the year 2020 (for industrialised economies, 2010) (*ASEAN Economic Bulletin* 1994) has challenged the ability of ASEAN to remain relevant.[1] At the same time, however, it is evident that the emergence of rival institutions has recently boosted the efforts by ASEAN to accelerate integration among its members.

On the whole, the ASEAN countries have been rather reserved as far as new forms of regional cooperation have been concerned, even if it is true that some initiatives have emanated from ASEAN itself. The reason for this caution is no doubt the risk for blurring the profile of ASEAN and for jeopardizing results already achieved within this organization in the field of trade policy (cf. Hoon 1990: 20–21; Lee 1991; see, however, the positive rhetoric in the Singapore declaration of 1992: *ASEAN Economic Bulletin* 1992b). While this may be an understandable point of view on the part of the governments, some theoretical work suggests that competition between international organizations and other international cooperation is in the interest of the citizens, since competition forces the organizations to take the citizens' interests seriously into account (Frey and Gygi 1991: 70–71). Indonesia has, as a rule, had the most favorable attitude, which possibly reflects the fact that the country is large in relation to ASEAN as a whole (cf. Ariff 1988: 167). The increasing interdependence in the Pacific region will make it difficult, and hardly even in the best interest of the member countries, for ASEAN to keep its distance from other regional organizations (cf. Yam et al. 1992). Indeed, a coherent ASEAN may be able to take advantage of the other regional organizations and wield considerable influence on them rather than be weakened by them.

## CONCLUSIONS

On balance, it may seem that ASEAN as an organization has not accomplished very much in the way of tangible results. According to this interpretation, the credit for the favorable economic development in the region cannot be given to ASEAN as an institution. What has been achieved in the strict realm of economic cooperation has, by and large, been related to pooling of resources, while sharing of markets has proved very difficult (cf. Akrasanee 1984: 32). In practice, it has not been possible to proceed faster than what the slowest member, usually Indonesia, has permitted. Still, as stressed by Wong (1989) ASEAN should be evaluated according to its own goals which are long-term ones. Hence a final evaluation is certainly premature. The gradual deepening of relations between the member countries is certainly something that will make future, more substantial, results possible. It is, however, more than likely that ASEAN's chief trade partners and foreign investors will continue in the foreseeable future to be nonmembers of the organization. Further economic integration should be planned in a way that does not disturb these relations.

Taking into account the great diversity of the members, the results produced by ASEAN are nevertheless respectable, even if the main achievements may not be in the realm of integrated economies. As Okamoto (1995) recently expressed it, the role of ASEAN from an economic point of view has been critical though passive. One of ASEAN's great achievements is that the organization evidently contributed to the absence of serious conflicts and to the political stability in the region. As far as foreign direct investors and aid donors are concerned, this is a result whose importance can hardly be overestimated. The member countries have also been able to concentrate more on their domestic development than what would otherwise have been the case. ASEAN has also become a respected actor on the international political scene with important, if unmeasurable, economic side effects. This may be instrumental for the future of wider cooperation schemes in the region, such as APEC as well, since the coordinated efforts of ASEAN make it a powerful force in the latter organization. The consultative style of ASEAN also suits a large and disparate organization like APEC quite well.

While the security-related argument for ASEAN has by no means disappeared, a stronger emphasis on the purely economic issues may be required for the organization to survive as an important regional actor in the long run perspective. Most of the cooperation programs from the 1970s and 1980s will probably not be viable in the long term (and actually seem to wither away quietly). In addition to developing the free trade area, there should be many openings for more limited concrete cooperation projects, for example, within the fields of education and technology, infrastructure, food security, and so on. In fact, many projects of this type are in operation already. In order to secure adequate support for the decision-making process, it would apparently be necessary to strengthen the role of the secretariat. A step toward this goal is the strengthening of the position of the secretary-general of the organization, decided at the Singapore Summit, who from now on will be appointed by merit, not according to the rotation principle (*Straits Times*, January 20, 1992; *New Straits Times*, January 20, 1992; *ASEAN Economic Bulletin* 1992a).

Returning, finally, to the question whether ASEAN can be considered a model for economic cooperation in other parts of the world, we note that the pure economic cooperation programs have had limited success so far. The process of cooperation has been characterized by consensus and flexibility, but also by unwillingness or inability to set up well-defined goals and schedules. This way of working, without overly ambitious goals at the outset, may be the main reason for the survival of the organization, but also the main reason for the lack of spectacular achievements (even if the positively developing relations no doubt lay a foundation for closer economic cooperation in the long run). It may well contain a lesson for other regional groupings in that it may not always be a good idea to start regional cooperation with too ambitious targets. A strong commitment to such goals leaves few ways out in a crisis and thus may cause a breakup of the organization instead. On the other hand, the ability to cooperate shown by the ASEAN nations can hardly be successfully copied mechanically. ASEAN's achievements may to a considerable extent be due to a unique combination of environmental circumstances and sheer personalities of the leaders in the different member countries. It would, for instance, be quite unthinkable to imagine ASEAN with an Indonesia led by President Sukarno. In the same vein, other similar "details" could easily have derailed the whole endeavor.

It has been argued, no doubt with some justification (see, e.g., Ariff 1992), that ASEAN's long-term vision is not very clear as to the forms its economic cooperation should take in the future. In the opinion of this author, it is likely, however, that the members will make serious efforts now in order to strengthen also the economic dimension of the organization. This is because a stronger ASEAN may be more effective within other, wider, organizations as a defender of the interests—not least the commercial interests—of its members than the latter could be on their own. In order to cope with that task, ASEAN cannot allow itself to be reduced to redundancy by other, partly overlapping organizations, such as APEC.

## NOTE

1. Despite this it is still unclear what will become of APEC. There is no any firm commitment to create a formal free trade area (*Economist,* September 16, 1995; see also Chapter 6 in this volume).

# 8

## Epilogue

The ascendance of the East Asian region toward a status of highly developed economies has been unprecedented although gradual. The process began in Japan, took off later in the NIEs, and eventually came to encompass the whole region, with few exceptions. Despite this, however, differences in income and general development levels are still very large, and only a rather small percentage of the population in the region has arrived at a stage of developed economy. During the process, the region has developed into a powerhouse for the global economy as well, with growth rates widely exceeding those reported from other parts of the world.

The crucial question for the future is, of course, whether the rapid development can be assumed to continue during the foreseeable future, until, say, 2020. With the benefit of hindsight, it is easy to see that Western economists and social scientists have been rather skeptical about the sustainability of this process all along, as if they had been looking for weaknesses in the Asian growth experience. This skepticism is still there, although it may take widely differing concrete forms. Clearly, however, a continuing favorable development cannot be taken for granted.

The hazards, as far as a strong future performance of East Asia is concerned, can be classified in three groups. First, the geopolitical and security situation in the region can easily change the outlook for future growth quite radically. Second, the social and political development within individual countries is bound to have an effect on the direction their economies will take. Finally, purely economic or economic-political realities may affect the outcome.

The first group is, paradoxically, both easy and hard to assess. On the one hand, it is clear that any serious disturbance in the security situation in the region, with a war as the ultimate case, would pose a very serious threat to prosperity in the region, although the effect is likely to be limited in time. It is also evident that such risks exist. In fact, apart from the Middle East, East Asia holds the greatest risks for armed conflicts in the world today. China is the potential flashpoint of all such possible conflicts (although only indirectly so in the case of the Koreas). Hence the development of the political situation in China is of utmost importance not only for that country itself but for all its neighbors as well. The problem is that it is extremely difficult to say anything about the probability of serious disturbances emanating from China, and even if that would be possible, to do anything about it. The de facto power vacuum after Deng Xiao-Ping appears not to be filled yet. Even if that part is handled satisfactorily, the tremendous social, political, and economic strain put on the country as a consequence of a rapid but uneven economic growth can cause major disruptions, for instance, in the form of uncontrolled migration.

The political development in the other East Asian countries is important as well but does not have the same type of international repercussions as in the case of China. In discussions on this issue, it often seems to be taken for granted that a convergence process toward a Western liberal democracy is taking place or, at least, should take place. This is by no means certain. In Asia a good deal of irritation is felt about the Western way of imposing its social values on other parts of the world. While some of this irritation may reflect the unwillingness of more or less authoritarian governments to relinquish power, some of it seems to have more profound reasons. Particularly the alleged lack of ability to balance the right of the individual and that of the society at large has been referred to, as has the (allegedly) detrimental consequences of welfare systems on morale and industriousness. Also the negative effects of rent-seeking special interests is a case in point, even if such interests are far from unknown also in East Asia. Authoritarian, or at least paternalistic, government has been referred to regularly in surveys on the reasons for the rapid development in the region (see, for instance, Tan 1992: 74–75). As for now, we do not know for sure whether the Asian countries in general will develop in the direction of more democratic systems or not, even if such a tendency is clear in some countries, such as the Philippines, Korea, and Taiwan.

While it is unclear how the political and social system in East Asia is going to develop, it is also far from certain what the economic effects of different alternatives would be. Even if different nuances of authoritarian government have dominated and still dominate in East Asia, the system is very different in different countries, and it is not easy to see a straightforward relation between economic development and degree of repressiveness. Indeed in Korea and Taiwan, a development toward a more democratic system does not seem to have hampered economic growth. The strength of an authoritarian (but developmental) government is probably its ability to take the long view and to keep the special interests at bay. On the other hand, repression may stifle development in the long term through different mechanisms, and in the end lead to eruptions of violence which would be harmful for economic development. As for democracy, it is perhaps more a weak and divided system without a strong and well-educated administrative bureaucracy that is detrimental for growth, more than democracy in itself.

As far as economic obstacles to growth are concerned, we may distinguish between problems in the international economic environment and purely domestic issues. It is obvious that the East Asian countries are dependent on a liberal international trading regime. This remains the case, even if the region now is much more self-sufficient than it used to be. This is also why the Asian countries have expressed so much worry about the recent tendency to form regional trade blocs. However, it is fair to say that despite these blocs, none of which is extremely  protectionist anyway, the world trading system has developed toward freer trade. There is no good reason now to assume that this trend will change radically during the next few decades. One risk factor is the high rates of unemployment, though, especially in Europe, which may induce governments to impose trade barriers as a desperate, but probably futile, attempt to counter the problem.

Another argument often invoked is that the growth of East Asia has been "factor driven," that is, driven by ever increasing quantities of capital and labor, while the role of increasing productivity has allegedly been minimal. Due to the problem of decreasing marginal returns, this would eventually lead to falling growth rates. This argument, while plausible in itself, suffers from the weakness of measurement problems, however, as demonstrated, for example, in a recent volume from the National Bureau of Economic Research (NBER) (Ito and Krueger 1995). Hence we do not actually know for sure how great the role of increasing productivity is and what the mechanisms are behind increasing productivity. Even if total productivity may have played a minor role before, it is not certain that this will be the case in the future either. Mobilizing labor and capital resources before concentrating on productivity-enhancing measures may have been perfectly rational at a certain stage of development. The Asian countries' heavy investment in education and vocational training seems to suggest that human capital will play a much more prominent role in the future, however. A fact that also seems to speak against the hypothesis of growth rates tapering off is the fact that countries like Korea, Singapore, and Taiwan have continued to grow rapidly even if they have reached very high levels of per capita income already. The most convincing argument in favor of continued rapid growth in the foreseeable future is the fact that most countries in the region, and, at the same time, the largest countries, are still at a low income level. Even with the problem of diminishing returns, they can go on growing rapidly for decades to come.

# References

Aitken, Norman D. "The Effect of the EEC and EFTA on European Trade: A Temporal Cross-Section Analysis," *American Economic Review*, 63, 1973.

Akamatsu, Kaname. "A Theory of Unbalanced Growth in the World Economy," *Weltwirtschaftliches Archiv*, 86, 1961.

————. "A Historical Pattern of Economic Growth in Developing Countries," *Developing Economies*, 1, 1962.

Akrasanee, Narongchai. ASEAN Economics and ASEAN Economic Cooperation. Manila: Asian Development Bank Economic Staff Paper No. 23, 1984.

Albrecht, Anthony C. "Economic Cooperation in the Asia-Pacific Region: The Southeast Asia Dimension." In Hardt, John P., and Kim, Young C. (eds.), *Economic Cooperation in the Asia-Pacific Region*. Boulder, Colo.: Westview Press, 1990.

Andersson, Thomas, and Burenstam Linder, Staffan. East Asian Development and Japanese Direct Investment. Working Paper No. 312. Stockholm: The Industrial Institute for Economic and Social Research, 1991.

Antolik, Michael. "ASEAN's Singapore Rendezvous: Just Another Summit?" *Contemporary Southeast Asia*, 14, 1992.

Anwar Nasution. "Aid and Development in ASEAN. Lessons from the 1980s." In Fukasaku, Kiichiro; Plummer, Michael; and Tan, Joseph (eds.), *OECD and ASEAN Economies. The Challenge of Policy Coherence*. Paris: OECD, 1995.

Ariff, Mohamed. "The Changing Role of ASEAN in the Coming Decades: Post-Manila Summit Perspectives." In Shinohara, Miyohei, and Lo Fu-chen (eds.), *Global Adjustment and the Future of Asian-Pacific Economy*. Kuala Lumpur and Tokyo: Institute of Developing Economies and the Asian and Pacific Development Centre, 1988.

————. *The Malaysian Economy. Pacific Connections*. Oxford and New York: Oxford University Press, 1991.

————. "Indonesia's Role as Big Brother," *Star*, January 25, 1992a.

————. "The Changing Role of ASEAN in the Coming Decades." In Sandhu, Kernial S., et al. (eds.), *The ASEAN Reader*. Singapore: Institute of Southeast Asian Studies, 1992b.

Ariff, Mohamed, and Tan Eu Chye. "ASEAN-Pacific Trade Relations," *ASEAN Economic Bulletin*, 8, 1992.

Ariff, Mohamed, and Tan, Joseph L. H. "Introduction," *ASEAN Economic Bulletin*, 8, 1992.

Arndt, Heinz W., and Garnaut, Ross. "ASEAN and the Industrialization of East Africa," *Journal of Common Market Studies*, 17, 1979.

Arndt, Sven W. "Industrial Structure, Competitiveness, and Trade," *North American Journal of Economics and Finance*, 1, 1990.

ASEAN. *AFTA Reader. Volume II. Questions and Answers on the CEPT for AFTA.* Jakarta: ASEAN Secretariat, 1995.

*ASEAN Economic Bulletin.* "Framework Agreement on Enhancing ASEAN Economic Cooperation," 8, 1992a.

————."Singapore Declaration 1992," 8, 1992b.

———— "Twenty-Sixth Meeting of the ASEAN Economic Ministers, Chiangmai, Thailand, 22–23 September 1994, Joint Press Statement," 11, 1994.

————. "APEC Economic Leaders' Declaration of Common Resolve. Bogor, Indonesia, 15 November 1994," 11, 1995.

———. "ASEAN Framework Agreement on Services," 12, 1996a.

———— "ASEAN Framework Agreement on Intellectual Property Cooperation," 12, 1996b.

*ASEAN Economic InfoView*, 1, No. 3, 1994.

*ASEAN Update,* July 1995.

*Asian Business*, various issues.

*Asian Business Review*, October 1995.

*Asiaweek*, 20, October 5 1994.

Balassa, Bela. *The Theory of Economic Integration.* London: George Allen and Unwin, 1961.

———. "Economic Integration." In Eatwell, John, et al. (eds.), *The New Palgrave. A Dictionary of Economics. Vol. 2, E to J.* London: Macmillan, 1988.

———. *Economic Policies in the Pacific Area Developing Countries.* Basingstoke and London: Macmillan, 1991.

Balassa, Bela, and Stoutjesdijk, Ardy. "Economic Integration among Developing Countries," *Journal of Common Market Studies*, 14, 1976.

Balasubramanyam, V. N.; Salisu, M.; and Sapsford, David. "Foreign Direct Investment and Growth in EP and IS Countries," *Economic Journal*, 106, 1996.

*Bangkok Post.* "Towards an ASEAN Economic Community," October 9, 1991.

Baum, Julian. "Taipei's Offshore Empire," *Far Eastern Economic Review*, March 18, 1993.

Bergsten, C. Fred. "An Asian Push for World-Wide Free Trade," *Economist*, January 6, 1996.

Bergsten, C. Fred, and Noland, Marcus. "Introduction and Overview." In Bergsten, C. Fred, and Noland, Marcus (eds.), *Pacific Dynamism and the International Economic System.* Washington, D.C.: Institute for International Economics, 1993.

Bhagwati, Jagdish N. "Directly Unproductive, Profit-Seeking (DUP) Activities," *Journal of Political Economy*, 90, 1978.

Blomqvist, Hans C. *Strukturomvandling och internationell konkurrenskraft* (Structural Change and International Competitiveness. With an English Summary). Research Reports 21. Helsinki: Swedish School of Economics and Business Administration, 1989.

———. "Structural Change and International Competitiveness: An Analysis of Adjustment in an Open Economy," *Journal of Economics and International Relations*, 3, 1990.

———. "ASEAN as a Model for Regional Economic Co-operation in the Third World?" *ASEAN Economic Bulletin*, 10, 1993.

Blomqvist, Hans C., and Lindholm, Christian. "The Economic Integration in Central America: Doomed to Fail?" *Ibero Americana*, 22, 1992.

Blomqvist, Hans C., and Lundahl, Mats. *Den snedvridna ekonomin*. Stockholm, SNS Förlag, forthcoming.

Blomqvist, Hans C.; Lindholm, Christian; Lundahl, Mats; and Schauman, Sven. "Some Experiences from Regional Cooperation between Third World Countries." In Odén, Bertil (ed.). *Southern Africa after Apartheid. Regional Integration and External Resources*. Uppsala, Sweden: The Scandinavian Institute of African Studies, 1993.

Blomqvist, Hans C., and Roy, Kartik C. Australian Exports to China: Can We Do Better? Paper presented at the International Conference on China and the Asia-Pacific Region, Brisbane, Australia, July 14–16, 1996.

Blomström, Magnus. *Foreign Investment and Spillovers*. London: Routledge, 1989.

———. *Transnational Corporations and Manufacturing Exports from Developing Countries*. New York: United Nations, 1990.

———. "Newly Emerging Technologies: Impact and Challenges for Developing Asian Countries." In Blomström, Magnus (ed.). *Transnational Technology towards the Year 2000 in the ESCAP Region*. New York: United Nations, 1994.

Brada, Josef C., and Mendez, José A. "Regional Economic Integration and the Volume of Intra-Regional Trade: A Comparison of Developed and Developing Country Experience," *Kyklos*, 36, 1983.

Bradford, Colin I., and Branson, William H. "Patterns of Trade and Structural Change." In Bradford, Colin I., and Branson, William H. (eds.), *Trade and Structural Change in Pacific Asia*. Chicago and London: University of Chicago Press, 1987.

Buckley, Peter J. "The Economic Analysis of the Multinational Enterprise: Reading versus Japan?" *Hitotsubashi Journal of Economics*, 26, 1985.

———. "Kojima's Theory of Japanese Foreign Direct Investment Revisited," *Hitotsubashi Journal of Economics*, 32, 1991.

Bulmer-Thomas, Victor. *Studies in the Economics of Central America*. Basingstoke and London: Macmillan, 1988.

Casson, Mark C. *The Firm and the Market. Studies on Multinational Enterprise and the Scope of the Firm*. Oxford: Basil Blackwell, 1987.

Cheeseman, Bruce. "Stop and Go in Korea," *Asian Business*, April 24, 1992.

Chen, Edward K. Y. "Foreign Direct Investment in East Asia," *Asian Development Review*, 11, 1993.

Chia Siow Yue. "Foreign Direct Investment in ASEAN Economies," *Asian Development Review*, 11, 1993.

Chia Siow Yue and Lee Tsao Yuan. "Subregional Economic Zones: A New Motive Force in Asia-Pacific Development." In Bergsten C. Fred, and Noland, Marcus (eds.), *Pacific Dynamism and the International Economic System*. Washington, D.C.: Institute for International Economics, 1993.

Chng Meng Kng. "ASEAN's Institutional Structure and Economic Cooperation," *ASEAN Economic Bulletin*, 6, 1990.

———. "Regional Business Development in ASEAN: The ASEAN Free Trade Area (AFTA)." In ASEAN. *AFTA Reader. Volume II. Questions and Answers on the CEPT for AFTA*. Jakarta: ASEAN Secretariat, 1995.

Chou Tein-Chen. "American and Japanese Direct Foreign Investment in Taiwan: A Comparative Study," *Hitotsubashi Journal of Economics*, 29, 1988.

Cohen, Benjamin. "The Triad and the Unholy Trinity: Lessons for the Pacific Region." In Higgott, Richard; Leaver, Richard; and Ravenhill, John (eds.),

*Pacific Economic Relations in the 1990s. Cooperation or Conflict?* St. Leonards, NSW: Allen & Unwin, 1993.

Colbert, Evelyn. "ASEAN as a Regional Organization: Economics, Politics, and Security." In Jackson, Karl J., et al. (eds.), *ASEAN in Regional and Global Context.* Berkeley: Institute of East Asian Studies, University of California, 1986.

Corden, W. Max. "Economies of Scale and Customs Union Theory," *Journal of Political Economy,* 80, 1972.

Cronin, Richard P. *Japan, the United States, and Prospects for the Asia-Pacific Century. Three Scenarios for the Future.* Singapore: Institute of Southeast Asian Studies, 1992.

Curry, Robert L., Jr. "Regional Economic Cooperation in Southern Africa and Southeast Asia," *ASEAN Economic Bulletin,* 8, 1991.

Daquila, Teofilo C., and Nguyen, D. T. "The Role of Northeast Asia in Singapore's Trade and Investment." In Nguyen, D. T., and Roy, K. C. (eds.), *Economic Reform, Liberalisation, and Trade in the Asia-Pacific Region.* New Delhi: Wiley Eastern, 1994.

Deardorff, Alan V. "Testing Trade Theories and Predicting Trade Flows." In Jones, Ronald W., and Kenen, Peter B. (eds.), *Handbook of International Economics, Volume I.* Amsterdam: North-Holland, 1984.

DeRosa, Dean. "Sources of Comparative Advantage in the International Trade of the ASEAN Countries," *ASEAN Economic Bulletin,* 10, 1993.

Devan, Janamitra. "The ASEAN Preferential Trading Agreement. Some Problems, Ex Ante Results, and a Multipronged Approach to Future Intra-ASEAN Trade Development," *ASEAN Economic Bulletin,* 4, 1987.

Dobson, Wendy. *Japan in East Asia. Trading and Investment Strategies.* Singapore: Institute of Southeast Asian Studies, 1993.

Drysdale, Peter. Japanese Foreign Investment in Australia in Comparative Perspective. Pacific Economic Papers No. 223. Canberra: Australia-Japan Research Centre, Australian National University, 1992.

East Asia Analytical Unit. ASEAN Free Trade Area. Trading Bloc or Building Bloc? Canberra: Department of Foreign Affairs and Trade, 1994.

Easterly, William. "Explaining Miracles: Growth Regressions Meet the Gang of Four." In Ito, Takatoshi, and Krueger, Anne O. (eds.), *Growth Theories in Light of the East Asian Experience.* Chicago and London: The University of Chicago Press, 1995.

*Economist.* "Regionalism and Trade. The Right Direction?" September 16, 1995.

———. "Making APEC Work," November 11, 1995.

———. "No Action, No Agenda," November 25, 1995.

El-Agraa, Ali M., and Jones, Anthony J. *The Theory of Customs Unions.* Oxford: Philip Allan, 1981.

Elek, Andrew. "The Challenge of Asian-Pacific Economic Cooperation," *Pacific Review,* 4, 1991.

———. "Trade Policy Options for the Asia-Pacific Region in the 1990s: The Potential of Open Regionalism," *American Economic Review,* 82, 1992.

———. "APEC beyond Bogor: An Open Economic Association in the Asian-Pacific Region," *Asian-Pacific Economic Literature,* 9, 1995.

ESCAP. *Economic and Social Survey of Asia and the Pacific.* Bangkok: Economic and Social Commission for Asia and the Pacific, 1994.

ESCAP. *Foreign Trade Statistics of Asia and the Pacific.* Bangkok: Economic and Social Commission for Asia and the Pacific, 1994.

*Far Eastern Economic Review.* "Action at Last," February 6, 1992.

Forbes, Alasdair. "Asia's Drive to Open Markets," *Asian Business,* 32, 1996.

Fratianni, M., and Pattison, J. "The Economics of International Organizations," *Kyklos*, 35, 1982.

Frey, Bruno S. *International Political Economics*. Oxford and Cambridge, Mass.: Basil Blackwell, 1984.

———. "The Public Choice View of International Political Economy." In Vaubel, Roland, and Willett, Thomas D. (eds.), *The Political Economy of International Organizations*. Boulder, Colo.: Westview Press, 1991.

Frey, Bruno S., and Gygi, Beat. "International Organizations from the Constitutional Point of View." In Vaubel, Roland, and Willett, Thomas D. (eds.), *The Political Economy of International Organizations*. Boulder, Colo.: Westview Press, 1991.

Frost, Frank. "Introduction: ASEAN since 1967—Origins, Evolution and Recent Developments." In Broinowski, Alison (ed.). *ASEAN into the 1990s*. Basingstoke and London: Macmillan, 1990.

GATT. *Trade Policy Review, Singapore. Vol. I*. Geneva: GATT, 1992.

Gill, Ranjit. *ASEAN Coming of Age*. Singapore: Sterling Corporate Services, 1987.

Government of the Republic of China. *Statistical Yearbook of the Republic of China*. Taipei: Directorate-General of Budget, Accounting and Statistics, Executive Yuan, 1990.

———. *Monthly Bulletin of Statistics of the Republic of China*. Taipei: Directorate-General of Budget, Accounting and Statistics, Executive Yuan, 1995.

———. *Monthly Statistics of the Republic of China*. Taipei: Directorate-General of Budget, Accounting and Statistics, Executive Yuan, July 1994.

Government of Singapore. *Singapore's Investment Abroad, 1976–1989*. Singapore: Department of Statistics, 1991.

Grant, Richard J.; Papadakis, Maria C.; and Richardson, J. David. "Global Trade Flows: Old Structures, New Issues, Empirical Evidence." In Bergsten, C. Fred, and Noland, Marcus (eds.), *Pacific Dynamism and the International Economic System*. Washington, D.C.: Institute for International Economics, 1993.

Greenaway, David, and Milner, Chris. *Trade and Industrial Policy in Developing Countries*. Basingstoke: Macmillan, 1993.

Grosser, Kate, and Bridges, Brian. "Economic Interdependence in East Asia: The Global Context," *Pacific Review*, 3, 1990.

Guisinger, Stephen. "Foreign Direct Investment Flows in East and Southeast Asia," *ASEAN Economic Bulletin*, 8, 1991.

Harris, Stuart. "Varieties of Pacific Economic Cooperation," *Pacific Review*, 4, 1991.

——— "Economic Cooperation and Institution Building in the Asia-Pacific Region." In Higgott, Richard; Leaver, Richard; and Ravenhill, John (eds.), *Pacific Economic Relations in the 1990s. Cooperation or Conflict?* St. Leonards, NSW: Allen & Unwin, 1993.

———. "Policy Networks and Economic Cooperation: Policy Coordination in the Asia-Pacific Region," *Pacific Review*, 7, 1994.

Hellmann, Donald C. America, APEC and the Road not Taken: International Leadership in the Post-Cold War Interregnum in the Asia-Pacific. Unpublished paper, University of Washington, 1995.

Higgott, Richard. "Economic Cooperation: Theoretical Opportunities and Practical Constraints," *Pacific Review*, 6, 1993.

Higgott, Richard; Leaver, Richard; and Ravenhill, John. "Introduction: Political Economy and the Pacific." In Higgott, Richard; Leaver, Richard; and Ravenhill, John (eds.), *Pacific Economic Relations in the 1990s. Cooperation or Conflict?* St. Leonards, NSW: Allen & Unwin, 1993.

Hill, Hal. "Foreign Investment and East Asian Economic Development," *Asian-Pacific Economic Literature*, 4, 1990.

Hill, Hal, and Johns, Brian. "The Role of Direct Foreign Investment in Developing East Asian Countries," *Weltwirtschaftliches Archiv*, 121, 1985.

Holden, Ted. "All Roads Lead to Tokyo," *International Business Week*, November 11, 1991.

Hong Wontack. "Export-Oriented Growth of Korea: A Possible Path to Advanced Economy," *International Economic Journal*, 4, 1990.

Hoon Khaw Guat. "The International Politics of Southeast Asia. Issues in 1989," *Southeast Asian Affairs*, 1990.

Hughes, Helen. "Does APEC Make Sense?" *ASEAN Economic Bulletin*, 8, 1991.

Hunt, Diana. *Economic Theories of Development: An Analysis of Competing Paradigms*. New York: Harvester Wheatsheaf, 1989.

Ichimura, Shinichi. "The Patterns and Prospects of Asian Economic Development." In Ichimura, Shinichi (ed.). *Challenge of Asian Developing Countries*. Tokyo: Asian Productivity Organization, 1988.

Imada, Pearl; Montes, Manuel; and Naya, Seiji. *A Free Trade Area. Implications for ASEAN*. Singapore: ASEAN Economic Research Unit, Institute of Southeast Asian Studies, 1992.

International Monetary Fund. *Directions of Trade Statistics*. Washington, D.C.: IMF, various years.

Ito, Takatoshi, and Krueger, Anne O. (eds.), *Growth Theories in Light of the East Asian Experience*. Chicago and London: The University of Chicago Press, 1995.

Jesudason, James V. *Ethnicity and the Economy. The State, Chinese Business, and Multinationals in Malaysia*. Singapore: Oxford University Press, 1989.

Johnson, Harry G. *Economic Policies toward Less Developed Countries*. Washington, D.C.: Brookings Institution, 1967.

Kaifu, Toshiki. "Japan and ASEAN: Seeking a Mature Partnership for the New Age," *ASEAN Economic Bulletin*, 8, 1991.

Kohama, Hirohisa. "Japan's Development Cooperation and Economic Development in Asia." In Ito, Takatoshi, and Krueger, Anne O. (eds.), *Growth Theories in Light of the East Asian Experience*. Chicago and London: University of Chicago Press, 1995.

Kohama, Hirohisa, and Teranishi, Juro. "Japan's ODA Policy and Economic Development of Recipient Countries." In Yamazawa, Ippei, and Hirata, Akira (eds.), *Development Cooperation Policies of Japan, the United States, and Europe*. Tokyo: Institute of Developing Economies, 1992.

Kojima, Kiyoshi. "A Macroeconomic Approach to Foreign Direct Investment," *Hitotsubashi Journal of Economics*, 14, 1973.

———. "International Trade and Foreign Investment: Substitutes or Complements?" *Hitotsubashi Journal of Economics*, 16, 1975.

———. *Japan and a New World Economic Order*. London: Croom Helm, 1977.

———. "Japanese and American Direct Investment in Asia: A Comparative Analysis," *Hitotsubashi Journal of Economics*, 26, 1985.

Kojima, Kiyoshi, and Ozawa, Terutomo. "Micro- and Macro-economic Models of Direct Investment toward a Synthesis," *Hitotsubashi Journal of Economics*, 25, 1984.

———. "Toward a Theory of Industrial Restructuring and Dynamic Comparative Advantage," *Hitotsubashi Journal of Economics*, 26, 1985.

Koppel, Bruce, and Plummer, Michael. "Japan's Ascendancy as a Foreign Aid Power: Asian Perspectives," *Asian Survey*, 24, 1989.

Korhonen, Pekka. *The Origin of the Idea of the Pacific Free Trade Area*. Jyväskylä, Finland: Jyväskylä Studies in Education, Psychology and Social Sciences, 92, University of Jyväskylä, 1992.

————. "The Theory of the Flying Geese Pattern of Development and Its Interpretations," *Journal of Peace Research*, 31, 1994.

Krueger, Anne O. *Growth, Distortions, and Patterns of Trade among Many Countries.* Princeton: Princeton Studies in International Finance No. 40, 1977.

————. *Political Economy of Policy Reform in Developing Countries.* Cambridge, Mass., and London: MIT Press 1993.

Krugman, Paul R. "Introduction: New Thinking about Trade Policy." In Krugman, Paul R. (ed.). *Strategic Trade Policy and the New International Economics.* Cambridge, Mass., and London: MIT Press, 1986.

————. "The Myth of Asia's Miracle," *Foreign Affairs,* 73, 1994.

Kumar, Sree. "Policy Issues and the Formation of the ASEAN Free Trade Area." In Imada, Pearl, and Naya, Seiji (eds.), *AFTA. The Way Ahead.* Singapore: Institute of Southeast Asian Studies, 1991.

————. "New Directions for Economic Growth in Southeast Asia," *Southeast Asian Affairs 1993,* 1993.

Kumar, Sree, and Siddique, Sharon. "Beyond Economic Reality: New Thoughts on the Growth Triangle," *Southeast Asian Affairs 1994,* 1994.

Kwan, C. H. *Economic Interdependence in the Asia-Pacific Region.* London and New York: Routledge, 1994.

Langhammer, Rolf J. "Trade in Manufactures between Asian Pacific Rim Countries," *ASEAN Economic Bulletin,* 6, 1989.

————. "ASEAN Economic Co-operation. A Stock-Taking from a Political Economy Point of View," *ASEAN Economic Bulletin,* 8, 1991a.

————. "Competition among Developing Countries for Foreign Investment in the Eighties—Whom Did OECD Investors Prefer?" *Weltwirtschaftliches Archiv,* 127, 1991b.

Langhammer, Rolf, and Hiemenz, Ulrich. *Regional Integration among Developing Countries: Opportunities, Obstacles and Options.* Tübingen: J.C.B. Mohr, 1990.

Leamer, Edward E. *Sources of International Comparative Advantage.* Cambridge, Mass.: MIT Press, 1984.

Leamer, Edward E., and Stern, Robert M. *Quantitative International Economics.* Boston: Allyn and Bacon, 1970.

Lee Chung H. "Direct Foreign Investment, Structural Adjustment, and International Division of Labor: A Dynamic Macroeconomic Theory of Direct Foreign Investment," *Hitotsubashi Journal of Economics,* 31, 1990.

Lee Tsao Yuan. ASEAN: Where Do We Go from Here? Some Thoughts on Economic Cooperation. Report No. 2. Singapore: The Institute of Policy Studies, 1991.

Leger, John M. "Come Together: Investment and Trade Links Are Growing Rapidly in Asia," *Far Eastern Economic Review,* 158, October 12, 1995.

Lewis, W. Arthur. "The Slowing Down of the Engine of Growth," *American Economic Review,* 70, 1980.

Lincoln, Edward J. "Japan's Role in Asia-Pacific Cooperation: Dimensions, Prospects, and Problems." In Hardt, John P., and Kim Young C. (eds.), *Economic Cooperation in the Asia-Pacific Region.* Boulder, Colo.: Westview Press, 1990.

Linnemann, Hans. *An Econometric Study of International Trade Flows.* Amsterdam: North-Holland, 1966.

Lipsey, Richard G. "The Theory of Customs Unions. Trade Diversion and Welfare," *Economica,* 24, 1957.

————. "The Theory of Customs Unions: A General Survey," *Economic Journal,* 70, 1960.

Lizondo, J. Saúl. "Foreign Direct Investment." In *Determinants and Systematic Consequences of International Capital Flows*. Occasional Paper 77. Washington, D.C.: IMF, 1991.

Lloyd, Peter J. "Intraregional Trade in the Asian and Pacific Region," *Asian Development Review*, 12, 1994.

Low, Linda. "The East Asian Economic Grouping," *Pacific Review*, 4, 1991.

Markusen, James R. "The Theory of the Multinational Enterprise: A Common Analytical Framework." In Ramstetter, Eric D. (ed.). *Direct Foreign Investment in Asia's Developing Economies and Structural Change in the Asia-Pacific Region*. Boulder, Colo.: Westview Press, 1991.

Meade, James. *The Theory of Customs Unions*. Amsterdam: North-Holland, 1955.

Meier, Gerald M. (ed.). *Leading Issues in Economic Development*. 5th ed. New York and Oxford: Oxford University Press, 1989.

Mortimore, Michael. "Flying Geese or Sitting Ducks? Transnationals and Industry in Developing Countries," *CEPAL Review*, 51, 1993.

Natarajan, S., and Tan Juay Miang. *The Impact of MNC Investments in Malaysia, Singapore and Thailand*. Singapore: ASEAN Economic Research Unit, Institute of Southeast Asian Studies, 1992.

Naya, Seiji, and Plummer, Michael G. "ASEAN Economic Co-operation in the New International Economic Environment," *ASEAN Economic Bulletin*, 7, 1991.

Naya, Seiji, and Ramstetter, Eric D. "Foreign Direct Investment in Asia's Developing Economies and Trade in the Asian and Pacific Region." In ESCAP. *Foreign Investment, Trade and Economic Cooperation in the Asian and Pacific Region*. Bangkok: Economic and Social Commission for Asia and the Pacific, 1992.

*New Straits Times*, various issues.

OECD. *International Investment and Multinational Enterprises. Recent Trends in International Direct Investment*. Paris: OECD, 1987.

————. *International Direct Investment and the New Economic Environment*. Paris: OECD, 1989.

Okamoto, Jiro. ASEAN's New Role in the Asia Pacific Region: Can It Be a Driving Force of Wider Regional Economic Cooperation? Pacific Economic Papers No. 245. Canberra: Australia-Japan Research Centre, 1995.

Olson, Mancur, and Zeckhauser, Richard. "An Economic Theory of Alliances," *Review of Economics and Statistics*, 48, 1966.

Ozawa, Terutomo. *Multinationalism, Japanese Style. The Political Economy of Outward Dependency*. Princeton: Princeton University Press, 1979.

Panagariya, Arvind. "East Asia and the New Regionalism in World Trade," *World Economy*, 17, 1994.

Peltola, Jari. Kojiman suhteellisten etujen hypoteesi suorille sijoituksille—kiista länsimaisen teorian universaalisuudesta. Discussion Papers No. 522. Helsinki, Finland: Research Institute of the Finnish Economy (ETLA), 1994.

Phongpaichit, Pasuk. *The New Wave of Japanese Investment in ASEAN*. Singapore: ASEAN Economic Research Unit, Institute of Southeast Asian Studies, 1990.

Porter, Michael E. *The Competitive Advantage of Nations*. London and Basingstoke: Macmillan, 1990.

Pöyhönen, Pertti. "A Tentative Model for the Value of Trade between Countries," *Weltwirtschaftliches Archiv*, 90, 1963.

Rafidah Aziz. "The Pacific and the International Trading System," *ASEAN Economic Bulletin*, 8, 1991.

Rahman Ibrahim, and Mansor Md. Isa. "Non-Tariff Barriers to Expanding Intra-ASEAN Trade," *ASEAN Economic Bulletin*, 4, 1987.

Rana, Pradumna. Recent Trends and Issues on Foreign Direct Investment in Asian and Pacific Developing Countries. Manila: Asian Development Bank Economic Staff Paper No. 41, 1988.

Rana, Pradumna B., and Dowling, J. Malcolm Jr. "Foreign Capital and Asian Economic Growth," *Asian Development Review*, 8, 1991.

Rapp, William V. "The Many Possible Extensions of Product Cycle Analysis," *Hitotsubashi Journal of Economics*, 16, 1975.

Reynolds, Clark W. Notes on the Enterprise for the Americas Initiative and the Andean Pact: Open Regionalism in the Andes. Working Paper 5/92. Stanford, Calif.: Stanford University, Americas Program, 1992.

Rhee Jong-Chan. *The State and Industry in South Korea. The Limits of the Authoritarian State*. London: Routledge, 1994.

Richardson, J. David. "'New' Trade Theory and Policy a Decade Old: Assessment in a Pacific Context." In Higgott, Richard; Leaver, Richard; and Ravenhill, John (eds.), *Pacific Economic Relations in the 1990s. Cooperation or Conflict?* St. Leonards, NSW: Allen & Unwin, 1993.

Riedel, J. "Economic Development in East Asia: Doing What Comes Naturally?" In Hughes, H. (ed.). *Achieving Industrialization in East Asia*. Cambridge: Cambridge University Press, 1988.

Rieger, Hans Christoph. "Regional Economic Co-operation in the Asia-Pacific Region," *Asian-Pacific Economic Literature*, 3, 1989.

———, (comp.). *ASEAN Economic Co-operation Handbook*. Singapore: Institute of Southeast Asian Studies, 1991.

Rix, Alan. "Japan's Foreign Aid Policy: A Capacity for Leadership," *Pacific Affairs*, 62, 1989/90.

———. "Japan and the Region: Leading from Behind." In Higgott, Richard, Leaver, Richard and Ravenhill, John (eds.), *Pacific Economic Relations in the 1990s. Cooperation or Conflict?* St Leonards, NSW: Allen & Unwin, 1993.

Robson, Peter. *The Economics of International Integration*. 2nd ed. London: George Allen and Unwin, 1984.

Rolls, Mark G. "ASEAN: Where from or Where to?" *Contemporary Southeast Asia*, 13, 1991.

Ruffin, Roy. "The Role of Foreign Investment in the Economic Growth of the Asian and Pacific Region," *Asian Development Review*, 11, 1993.

Savage, I. R., and Deutsch, K. W. "A Statistical Model of the Gross Analysis of Transaction Flows," *Econometrica*, 28, 1960.

*Singapore*. "Contributing to the Global Society," May/June, 1993.

Singer, Hans W. and Alizadeh, Parvin. Import Substitution Revisited in a Darkening External Environment. UNCTAD Working Paper I/2, 1986.

Södersten, Bo, and Reed, Geoffrey. *International Economics*. 3rd ed. Basingstoke and London: Macmillan, 1994.

Srinivasan, T. N. (ed.). *Agriculture and Trade in China and India*. San Francisco: ICEG, 1994.

Steven, Rob. *Japan and the New World Order. Global Investments, Trade and Finance*. Basingstoke: Macmillan, 1996.

*Straits Times*, various issues.

*Straits Times*, Weekly Edition, August 12, 1995.

Suriyamongkol, Marjorie L. *Politics of ASEAN Economic Co-operation. The Case of ASEAN Industrial Projects*. Oxford: Oxford University Press, 1988.

Tan, Gerald. *The Newly Industrializing Countries of Asia*. Singapore: Times Academic Press, 1992.

Thambipillai, Pushpa, and Saravanamuttu, Johan. *ASEAN Negotiations. Two Insights.* Singapore: Institute of Southeast Asian Studies, 1985.

Tinbergen, Jan. *Shaping the World Economy: Suggestions for an International Economic Policy.* New York: The Twentieth Century Fund, 1962.

Tran Van Tho. "Foreign Capital and Technology in the Process of Catching Up by the Developing Countries: The Example of Synthetic Fiber Industry in the Republic of Korea," *Developing Economies,* 26, 1988.

*Transnationals* (Quarterly Newsletter of the United Nations Centre on Transnational Corporations), 3, No. 4 (December), 1991.

UNCTAD, Division on Transnational Corporations and Investment. "World Investment Report 1994: Transnational Corporations, Employment, and the Workplace. An Executive Summary," *Transnational Corporations,* 3, 1994.

UNIDO. *Foreign Direct Investment Flows to Developing Countries. Recent Trends, Major Determinants and Policy Implications.* Geneva: UNIDO, 1990.

Union of International Associations. *Yearbook of International Organizations 1995/96, Vol. 1.* Munich: KG. Saur, 1995.

United Nations. "Economic Co-operation for ASEAN," *Journal of Development Planning,* 7, 1974.

————. *World Investment Report. The Triad of Foreign Direct Investment.* New York: UN, 1991.

————. *The Determinants of Foreign Direct Investment: A Survey of the Evidence.* New York: UN, 1992a.

————. *World Investment Directory. Vol. I. Asia and the Pacific.* New York: UN, 1992b.

————. *World Investment Directory. Volume III. Developed Countries.* New York: UN, 1993.

————. *Energy Statistics Yearbook.* New York: UN, various years.

————. *National Accounts Statistics.* New York: UN, various years.

Urata, Shujiro. "The Rapid Increase of Direct Investment Abroad and Structural Change in Japan." In Ramstetter, Eric D. (ed.). *Direct Foreign Investment in Asia's Developing Economies and Structural Change in the Asia-Pacific Region.* Boulder, Colo.: Westview Press, 1991.

————. "Changing Patterns of Direct Investment and the Implications for Trade and Development." In Bergsten C. Fred, and Noland, Marcus (eds.), *Pacific Dynamism and the International Economic System.* Washington, D. C.: Institute for International Economics, 1993.

USIS. *Economic Backgrounder.* Hong Kong: USIS, 1994.

Vaitsos, Constantine. "Crisis in Regional Economic Cooperation (Integration) among Developing Countries: A Survey," *World Development,* 6, 1978.

Vanek, Jaroslav. "The Factor Proportions Theory: The N-Factor Case," *Kyklos,* 21,1968.

Vatikiotis, Michael. "Action at Last," *Far Eastern Economic Review,* February 6, 1992.

Vaubel, Roland. "A Public Choice View of International Organization." In Vaubel, Roland, and Willett, Thomas D. (eds.), *The Political Economy of International Organizations.* Boulder, Colo.: Westview Press, 1991.

Vernon, Raymond. "International Investment and International Trade in the Product Cycle," *Quarterly Journal of Economics,* 80, 1966.

Viner, Jacob. *The Customs Union Issue.* New York: Carnegie Endowment for International Peace,  1950.

Waitt, Gordon. "The Composition and Direction of the Republic of Korea's Outward Foreign Direct Investment," *Asian Profile,* 21, 1993.

Wong, Douglas. "Cheow Tong Backs Implementing AFTA by 2000," *Straits Times*, Weekly Edition, September 2, 1995.

Wong, John. "ASEAN's Experience in Regional Economic Co-operation," *Asian Development Review*, 3, 1985.

———. "The ASEAN Model of Regional Cooperation." In Naya, Seiji, et al. (eds.), *Lessons in Development. A Comparative Study of Asia and Latin America*. Panama City: International Center for Economic Growth, 1989.

Woods, Lawrence T. "Non-governmental Organizations and Pacific Cooperation: Back to the Future?" *Pacific Review*, 4, 1991.

World Bank. *World Development Report*. New York: Oxford University Press, various years.

———. *World Tables*. Baltimore and London: Johns Hopkins University Press, various years.

———. *East Asia's Trade and Investment. Regional and Global Gains from Liberalization*. Washington, D.C.: World Bank, 1994.

Wysocki, Bernhard Jr. "In Asia, the Japanese Hope to 'Coordinate' What Nations Produce," *Wall Street Journal*, August 20, 1990.

Yam Tan Kong; Heng Toh Mun; and Low, Linda. "ASEAN and Pacific Economic Cooperation," *ASEAN Economic Bulletin*, 8, 1992.

Yamazawa, Ippei. *Economic Development and International Trade. The Japanese Model*. Honolulu: East-West Center, 1990.

Young Soogil. "Globalism and Regionalism: Complements or Competitors?" In Bergsten, C. Fred, and Noland, Marcus (eds.), *Pacific Dynamism and the International Economic System*. Washington, D.C.: Institute for International Economics, 1993.

# Index

**About the Author**

HANS C. BLOMQVIST is Associate Professor of Economics at the Swedish School of Economics and Business Administration in Vasa, Finland. Dr. Blomqvist is the author or editor of numerous journal articles and five books including *Economic Development and Women in the World Community* (Praeger, 1996).

ISBN 0-275-95583-4

90000>

9 780275 955830

EAN

HARDCOVER BAR CODE